Divine Synchronicity

Women's Stories of
MAGIC, MIRACLES & MANIFESTING

Compiled by Linda Joy
Edited by Deborah Kevin and Linda Dessau

A Sacred Gift
to Support You on Your Self-Discovery Journey

Discover the power of energy-infused affirmations to elevate your mindset and create your intentional life.

Mindset Elevation *Intentional Life* Screensaver Set

Your Mindset Elevation Affirmation Screensaver Set includes:

~5 energy-infused affirmation screensavers for your desktop or laptop

~5 energy-infused affirmation screensavers for your phone.

~Invitation to the Inspiration Lounge™ Facebook community

~VIP notice on future complimentary 5-day Mindset Elevation Soul Camps™

It's time to say yes to igniting your inner mojo and to living an intentional life!

Download your complimentary gift at:
www.MindsetElevationGiftSet.com

DIVINE SYNCHRONICITY Copyright @2024 Linda Joy.

All rights reserved. The contents of this book may not be transmitted or reproduced in any form or by any means, mechanical or electronic, including photocopying, recording or by any information storage and retrieval system, without prior written permission from the author, with the exception only of the inclusion of brief quotations in a review.

In some cases, names and identifying information has been changed to protect client privacy.

ISBN: 979-8-9911626-0-9
ebook ISBN: 979-8-9911626-1-6
Library of Congress Control Number: Applied for

Published by Inspired Living Publishing, LLC.
P.O. Box 1149, Lakeville, MA 02347

Cover and interior design: Lisa Hromada (www.LoveIsTheSeed.com)
Interior layout: Patricia Creedon (www.PatCreedonDesign.com)
Managing Editor: Deborah Kevin, MA (www.DeborahKevin.com)
Associate Editor: Linda Dessau (www.LDEditorial.com)
Linda Joy photo credit: Ali Rosa Photography (www.AliRosaPhotography.com)

Dedication

This book is dedicated to:

The loves of my life:
Dana, Niki, Makenna, Glenn, and Tyler,
My life is richer because of each of you.

As well as:

The authors of *Divine Synchronicity*:

Thank you for entrusting me, and the Inspired Living Publishing team, with your sacred soul story. I honor your willingness to dive deep as you were guided through the Authentic Storytelling™ process and your courage in sharing your most vulnerable and heart-opening moments with the intention to support and inspire other women on their journey.

My magical team and collaborators on this project:

Deborah Kevin, chief editor on this sacred project, who brings the essence of each story to light and who compassionately holds space for our authors to share their truth.

Linda Dessau, associate editor for holding loving space for their stories to be told.

Lisa Hromada for the stunning soul-inspiring cover and interior design.

Patricia Creedon for the interior content layout.

Kim Turcotte, my Goddess of Operations and soul sister, who organizes and brings my visions to life.

And finally…to you the reader:

May these stories remind you to keep your eyes, and heart, open for the signs, magic and miracles all around you.

Inspired Living Publishing's bestselling titles include:

The Art of Self-Nurturing: A Field Guide to Living with More Peace, Joy & Meaning by Kelley Grimes, MSW

Broken Open: Embracing Heartache and Betrayal as Gateways to Unconditional Love by Mal Duane

Soul-Hearted Living: A Year of Sacred Reflections & Affirmations for Women by Dr. Debra Reble

Everything Is Going to Be Okay!: From the Projects to Harvard to Freedom by Dr. Catherine Hayes, CPCC

Being Love: How Loving Yourself Creates Ripples of Transformation in Your Relationship and the World by Dr. Debra Reble

Awakening to Life: Your Sacred Guide to Consciously Creating a Life of Purpose, Magic, and Miracles by Patricia Young;

The Art of Inspiration: An Editor's Guide to Writing Powerful, Effective Inspirational & Personal Development Books, by Bryna Haynes.

As well as these bestselling titles in our sacred anthology division:

Life Shifts: Women's Stories of Surrendering to and Rising Above Life's Challenges

Reclaiming Your Midlife Mojo: Women's Stories of Self-Discovery & Transformation

Life Reimagined! Women's Stories of Hope, Resilience & Transformation

SHINE! Stories to Inspire You to Dream Big, Fear Less & Blaze Your Own Trail

Courageous Hearts: Soul-Nourishing Stories to Inspire You to Embrace Your Fears and Follow Your Dreams

Midlife Transformation: Redefining Life, Love, Health and Success

Inspiration for a Woman's Soul: Opening to Gratitude & Grace

Inspiration for a Woman's Soul: Cultivating Joy

Inspiration for a Woman's Soul: Choosing Happiness

Embracing Your Authentic Self: Women's Stories of Self-Discovery & Transformation

A Juicy, Joyful Life: Inspiration from Women Who Have Found the Sweetness in Every Day

Unleash Your Inner Magnificence (ebook only)

The Wisdom of Midlife Women 2 (ebook only)

You can find most of the titles at major online retailers and bookstores by request.

PRAISE FOR

Divine Synchronicity

"Each of us has powers far beyond our imagination, but we live in a world that insists we be 'realistic.' I love the stories in this book because they are so real—and will help you trust more in absolute divine connection. Read this book now and watch your doubts evaporate and your awe intensify."

TAMA KIEVES
Bestselling author of *A Year Without Fear* and
internationally popular teacher of *A Course in Miracles*

"The soul-nourishing stories featured in *Divine Synchronicity* will remind you that magic and miracles are all around you! When we stay open to the signs and synchronicities that appear on our path, as these women did, we'll discover that even in your darkest times, you are being lovingly guided and reminded that light, love, and possibility are always available to us. Allow these wisdom-filled stories to soothe your soul, expand your heart, and remind you of your truth and power. Enjoy."

CHRISTY WHITMAN
New York Times bestselling author of
The Art of Having It All

"*Divine Synchronicity* is yet another masterpiece of Linda Joy's collaborative spirit. The stories these women tell remind us of the sacred magic we all hold inside and call us to reclaim our own divine nature."

KIM CHESTNEY
Founder of IntuitionLab
and author of *The Illumination Code* and *Radical Intuition*

"We are always being divinely guided. Our role is to be present enough in our lives to see the signs and synchronicities all around us. The soul-inspiring stories of the women featured in *Divine Synchronicity* will remind you that magic and miracles are all around you and that we all have access to that flow of sacred energy. A must-read book for women ready to open themselves to possibility!"

AMY LEIGH MERCREE
Medical intuitive and bestselling author of eighteen books,
including *Aura Alchemy* and the card deck *Blissful Baths*

"*Divine Synchronicity: Women's Stories of Magic, Miracles & Manifesting* is a captivating anthology that beautifully illustrates the transformative power of paying attention to life's subtle signs. Each story serves as a testament to the everyday miracles that occur when we're open to the magic and mystery life has to offer."

KRISTI LING SPENCER
Bestselling author and host of The Joy School Podcast

"An inspirational delight! Grab a cup of your favorite beverage and curl up to nourish your soul as you journey through each author's heart-opening story. I love the self-reflection questions, too. *Divine Synchronicity* is a must-read for anyone craving more joy, magic, and connection. What a treasure!"

KIM COOTS
Sacred Empowerment coach

"I love this book! We are all more tapped into higher wisdom than we could ever know. We play the divine game of hide and seek, forgetting and remembering, feeling lost, and then, ultimately, feeling found. For any woman who has ever doubted herself and needs a reassuring friend to remind her of how powerful she is, *Divine Synchronicity: Women's Stories of Magic, Miracles, and Manifesting*, is that friend, that wakeup call, and that loving hug, reminding us we live in a friendly universe, and that we can trust ourselves, when it matters most."

KELLY SULLIVAN WALDEN
Bestselling author of *A Crisis Is a Terrible Thing to Waste*

"*Divine Synchronicity* is inspirational and thought-provoking! I loved these stories! Each one provides its own inspiration and makes you smile and feel deeply. I love that each story offers reflections afterward for you to think about and journal about. Synchronicity presents itself in so many different ways in our lives; these stories are beautiful examples. I see going back to these stories and prompts. The more we delve into these real-life stories of synchronicity, the more we prove it to ourselves and open ourselves up to it in our own lives. Each author has a unique voice and powerful experience to share. I am thrilled to have read this, will recommend it, and get it for friends."

JENNY GARUFI
Author and speaker

"A rich anthology where gifted women entrepreneurs share stories of discovering their innate gifts, connecting with their intuition, and learning to trust in the Universe. Reflection questions encourage us to go inside, connect with our unique gifts, and trust in the Universe. I highly recommend this book to any woman who wants to learn how to connect with her intuition and listen to and trust in the messages she is sent."

PAMELA THOMPSON
Founder of Female Wave of Change Canada and bestselling author of
Learning to Dance with Life and *The Exploits of Minerva*

"*Divine Synchronicity* is an insightful book of women's stories that speak to your soul. Each story reminds you to listen and trust the guidance and signs you receive because it can open up a whole new level in your life. Find your favorite chair and enjoy!"

MARY BETH GUDEWICZ
Board certified in holistic nutrition and intuitive healthy gut specialist

"*Divine Synchronicity* brings together inspiring stories of women tuning into their intuitive wisdom and inner knowing. These synchronistic moments lead them forward in compelling ways. This book is a must-read for those ready to uplift their inner journey."

LISA MICHAELS
Nature Aligned Prosperity mentor for today's leaders

Divine Synchronicity

"Once I started paying attention to the synchronicities that were all around me, my whole existence began to feel so aligned with something so much more vibrant! I highly recommend this beautiful book for everyone open to connecting themselves into a greater platform where magic and joy abound."

EMILY A. FRANCIS
Wellness advocate, radio host, and author of
The Taste of Joy: Mediterranean Wisdom for a Life Worth Savoring

Foreword

SHERIANNA BOYLE

Have you ever read a good story or had something happen to you that made you think about it throughout the rest of the day? Maybe you even shared what happened with others? This is one of the ways you know when an experience influences how you think, feel, and behave. For some of you, this may be all it takes to shift an attitude, perception, or belief. So often, it is all about timing. The way a sequence of events can line up in a certain way at a certain moment in time is *divine synchronicity.*

What makes these moments so powerful is their ability to evoke emotion. A feeling sparks inside you, bringing you into rather than away from the present moment, where all past experiences and traumas can be dissolved, transformed, and released; *this is magic.*

The Swiss psychologist and psychiatrist Carl Jung first coined the concept of synchronicity. He described it as "the meaningful coincidence of two or more events where something other than the probability of chance is involved." For example, when one of my dear friends lost her mother, within days after her passing, my friend walked into a store and got an overwhelming smell of her mother's perfume. Someone in the store was wearing it. Was that a coincidence or a sign that her mother was present? Divine synchronicity will always have its way of getting you to pay attention to the here and now.

The fact that I am writing the foreword to this book is another example of divine synchronicity. Writing this foreword was never on my radar, yet it arrived through a series of unforeseen circumstances. What I love about divine synchronicity is it always comes with the opportunity to feel, learn, and grow. For example, if you watch a movie or read a story, you may identify with the characters and events. When stories such as those in this book are told with integrity, awareness, and authenticity, it helps you process the events in your life and discover how divine synchronicity may be at work. If you have ever wondered whether your position at a certain moment happened by chance or on purpose, you know what I mean.

Maybe you have had unexpected changes, opportunities, and even challenges in your life. Whether you liked it or not, these events forced you to modify, alter, or even pause the path you were on. While it might have thrown you off balance at the time, you will soon see through the lens of storytelling how these twists and turns can often come with blessings.

Within this book's pages are examples of how divine synchronicity works. Some authors share how synchronicity arrived with some unexpected challenges, while others describe the comfort, reassurance, and fortitude it provided at the exact time they needed it. Throughout it all, you will see how divine synchronicity reminds us we are never alone.

Yet, so often, it can be tempting to judge, question, or minimize the signs and synchronicities that come our way. Perhaps there is a part of us that is not ready to receive them. What I have learned is judgment can spoil the magic. Similar to being in a relationship where two people criticize each other, this can cause the chemistry between the two to fade. Rest assured, reading stories like the ones in this book can help you dissolve these tendencies, helping you rekindle your relationship with yourself, others, and your spiritual team.

Yes, believe it or not, we all have a spiritual team that loves us unconditionally. If you are having difficulty connecting to your team, the reflective questions at the end of each chapter will help. It is through self-awareness these connections strengthen. Therefore, I highly encourage you to have a notebook handy as you move through the chapters of this book. These exercises can help you get out of your head and into your heart. As this occurs, you will naturally become more attentive to the signs and messages around you.

I must confess there have been times in my life when I resisted divine synchronicity. I cared more about the meaning than the message. For example, I might have overindulged in Googling (searching) for answers. Maybe I saw numbers repeated (like 777 or 555) on a license plate and found myself rushing to uncover the answers. While it can be fun to look up the many ways the universe speaks to us, I have learned that at some point, you will have to learn to trust and follow your intuition. Pay attention to how some authors handled these random coincidences in their own lives.

I also encourage you to let go of the need to analyze or examine the order in which things happen to you. This is because, unlike humans who like to operate off time by placing things in chronological order (e.g., when I am thirty, retired, married, etc., then I will do….), the universe doesn't function this way. Instead, it operates off divine order. It does this by linking the experiences your soul came here to learn so you can gain the knowledge and wisdom you need to evolve and fulfill your soul's mission on earth.

Therefore, dear soul friend, do your best to relinquish fear and instead put faith in your path. Know that behind the scenes, divine synchronicity is always at work. Let go of the how, what, when, and what ifs, and instead take a deep breath. This will help you lean into the process.

It is no accident you were drawn to this book. Some of you may even feel it arrived at exactly the time you needed it, which would

FOREWORD

mean you are, in fact, experiencing divine synchronicity. If so, I say slow down, sift through the stories at your own pace, and trust them because you are choosing to focus on divine synchronicity, and more messages, signs, and happenings orchestrated by the universe are coming.

With Love,
Sherianna Boyle
Author of eleven books, including the upcoming
Just Ask Spirit: Free Your Emotions to Energize Intuition &
Discover Purpose

Divine Synchronicity

Table of Contents

FOREWORD BY SHERIANNA BOYLE — xv

INTRODUCTION — 1

CHAPTER ONE | Embracing an Elevated Mindset

Undeniable Evidence — 7
Nancy OKeefe

Uncovering Gems on a Career Path — 13
Felicia Messina-D'Haiti

Divine Peace — 19
Wioleta Kapusta

The Labyrinth — 25
Crystal Cockerham

Serendipity and the Path to Mindful Gratitude — 33
Judy Gallauresi

From Crossroads to Clarity: Discovering Divine Guidance — 41
Sharon Seaberg

CHAPTER TWO | Soul Nudges to Reclaimed Health

Navigating Life's Challenges with Resilience — 51
Brenda Reimer-Harder

The Bear Story
Sara Gomez   59

Kintsugi: A Goddess in the Making
Tywanah Evette   67

CHAPTER THREE | Divinely Guided Relationships

Struck by Serendipity
Barb Pritchard   77

A Bouquet of White Flowers
Efrat Shokef   83

The Birthday Card
Yvette LeFlore   91

Divine Miracles: God's Perfect Timing
Donna Burgher   97

Angel in Disguise
Dawn Michele Jackson   105

I Got You
Carolyn Marie   111

Finding Self Love
Laurie Burkhalter   117

CHAPTER FOUR | Following Signs & Synchronicities

Consciously Orchestrating a Life-Changing Move
Karen Shier   125

Braving Wings
Amber Kasic   133

Bashert Amy Lindner-Lesser	141
Embracing that I'm a Teacher Robin Fitzsimons	149
A Big Loving Shove Toward Destiny Lisa Hromada	157
The Divine Hand Leads Me Home Bonnie Snyder	165
How I Became a Radio Psychic Sha Blackburn	173
EDITOR'S NOTE	179
ABOUT OUR AUTHORS	181
ABOUT OUR PUBLISHER	193
ABOUT OUR EDITOR	195

Introduction

I am a recovering "Micromanager of the Divine."

For the first three decades of my life, I embraced that title fully—and had the proverbial T-shirt, too.

Due to previous experiences, I held so tightly to every aspect of life—and lived under the illusion that I was in control. I falsely believed doing so would keep me emotionally, physically, and spiritually safe—and keep heartache, betrayal, struggle, and pain at bay.

The truth is that holding on so tightly kept me from experiencing the joy, love, abundance, and inner peace that I yearned for.

Deep down, I knew there was another way, but I hadn't yet opened my eyes and heart to see it. That was until a life-changing dark night of the soul in 1991.

On a spring day that year, which I wrote about in the introduction to Inspired Living Publishing's first book, *A Juicy, Joyful Life*, I awakened to the truth that by holding on so tightly, I energetically blocked the flow of all my desires and healing.

During that experience, I heard a stern but gentle and loving whisper that would transform my life, heal my heart, and allow me to dance with my authentic self for the first time. I heard,

INTRODUCTION

"The experiences of your childhood do not erase the core of who you are. You have been here all along but have chosen not to see yourself. Instead, you've focused on the pain. You hold the power to become, at any time, whatever you desire to be. You can choose to live in the past, with all your pain and anger, or you can choose to be the bright, beautiful person at the core of who you are right now. So, what will you choose?"

Epiphany!

I still remember the peace and energy that flowed through my body at that moment. Suddenly, I went from feeling helpless and lost to my heart being filled with pure hope—a feeling I hadn't experienced in a long, long time. The wisdom I heard that day, over thirty-three years ago, resonated deeply within my heart and on a soul level, reminding me of what I'd known, deep down, all along—I am always divinely supported. That spring day, I took back my life and opened my heart to trusting the Divine.

I began playing with the energy of trusting in the Divine. I began playing with the Divine—like a game. I'd ask for three signs or synchronicities to show me that I was being divinely supported. (Yes, I was still micromanaging the divine by asking for exact signs.)

As I softened into this new energy, I felt more open to life—to love, to my sense of trust in myself and the Divine. My spirit became lighter, and my heart started healing.

Soon, it became second nature to believe in possibility and to see the blessings, abundance, love, and support that were all around me.

A few years later, I realized that all those things I yearned for had always been available to me—but in 'micromanaging the divine,' I had closed myself off so rigidly that I couldn't see or experience them.

Decades later, I live my life believing that I am *a.l.w.a.y.s.* divinely supported—and magic, miracles, and blessings flow in. That doesn't mean that life doesn't throw me curveballs or difficult times—that's life! For me, it means that I now have a deeper sense of trust that even in difficult times—I am being supported.

Late last year, I received a nudge that Inspired Living Publishing's twenty-first book title would be *"Divine Synchronicity,"* and it resonated on a soul level.

My vision was to create a sacred compilation of women's stories that would inspire women to believe in possibility, open their hearts to letting go of what no longer served them, and remind them that signs and synchronicities are always guiding them—that vision is now in your hands.

Our collective intention is that the twenty-three women's stories will remind you, and all women, that everything you yearn for is in your energy field. Our role is to remain open, let go of control of micromanaging the divine, and open our hearts to seeing and believing that we're always divinely supported.

May their intimate stories and the journal prompts that invite you to dive deeper into your truth remind you to open to the magic, miracles, and abundance all around you.

I have replaced that T-shirt I once proudly wore with one that says, "I Trust that I am Divinely Supported."

Wishing you magic, miracles, and love.

Live an Intentional Life,

Linda Joy
Mindset Elevation Coach
Storytelling Guide and Bestselling Publisher
www.Linda-Joy.com

CHAPTER ONE

Embracing an Elevated Mindset

Undeniable Evidence

NANCY OKEEFE

It had been a long day with my office door closed and my head down, trying desperately to finish the report I had been putting together all week. I had eaten lunch at my desk again. It was important to me to make this report showcase the great work my department was doing in creating new functionality for the flagship software product the company sold. We had a lot to be proud of and my people deserved recognition for their innovative hard work.

My eyes were tired from staring at the computer screen all day, but they noticed the fading light outside my office window. I stopped to look at my watch. Ugh, only four o'clock in the afternoon and already getting dark!

I hated this time of year in New England. There just wasn't enough daylight. It was cold and dark when I got up for work in the morning and cold and dark when I got home in the evening. Thank goodness we had the holiday season to brighten up this dreary time of year. I did enjoy gawking at the holiday lights on the way home, especially the ones on Montgomery Drive. Everyone decorated their homes in that neighborhood. Some even had Christmas music playing. I was deep in a daydream about it. "Okay, Nancy, snap out of it and get back to work!" I said out loud. "You have an hour left in the day, and you can finish this report if you focus." So, I settled into my chair, took a sip of tea from my lunch, now stone cold, and proceeded to wrap up the report.

A few moments later I was jolted out of my work by a clear picture of our Christmas tree falling on my daughter. It popped into my head out of nowhere! I saw the tree fall on her as clearly as if it was happening in my office, with ornaments flying everywhere. I felt an immediate sense of panic and fear. "Ridiculous," I told myself, "It's just because you were thinking about Christmas lights. What an imagination you have!" My first reaction was to dismiss it. "What a stupid thing to think," I told myself. I went back to my work. I only had one more page of the report to complete and I could easily finish that before five, leave work on time, and get home to quell my fears.

My daughter was thirteen and home alone in the afternoon every day after school. I was a widowed single mom and although it wasn't ideal, it couldn't be helped. She was a good kid, got good grades, was trustworthy and capable, and we had rules to keep her safe. No one was allowed in, the door was locked, and she didn't go out until I got home. She would spend her afternoons doing her homework, watching TV, and talking on the phone with her friends—not necessarily in that order. I lived close to the office, so it took me no time at all to get home. Even so, I never felt good about leaving her alone.

As hard as I tried to finish that last page of the report, something kept nagging at me. I couldn't get the picture of the Christmas tree out of my head. What was I going to do? Go to my boss and tell him I had to leave early because I saw our Christmas tree fall on my daughter's head? He'd think I was crazy! So, I took a deep breath and got back to that last page of the report. Now it had become more about watching the clock get closer to five than finishing the report.

I'd had visions pop into my mind's eye many times before.

Usually, I dismissed them because they didn't make any sense to me, and I wasn't sure what else to do with them. I have known from an early age that I had some of the *clairs*: clairvoyance, clairaudience, and clairsentience. As a child, I tried to tell my mother what I saw and heard, even smelled, but she always told me I was being silly and to stop making things up in that wild imagination of mine. I learned to keep my clairs to myself and eventually stopped paying much attention to them. It became part of everyday life to smell my grandfather's pipe or my deceased husband's cigarettes, hear people talking to each other, or see pictures in my head. I guess I didn't realize everyone didn't experience that.

This time was quite different. The picture and the nagging feeling wouldn't be dismissed. I was clear about what this meant and what I was supposed to do with this information. This was about protecting and helping my child. The urge to go home was intense. After an agonizing thirty-five minutes, at 4:40 p.m., I packed up my desk and my laptop and trotted out the door. I'd finish the report at home after I made sure my daughter was okay.

The twenty-minute drive seemed like hours. I was intensely focused on getting home as quickly as possible. I forgot all about looking at the Christmas lights; the only lights I noticed were the red traffic lights. Why does it seem like you get every red when you are in a hurry? Finally, I turned onto Route 80 and drove the last half-mile to my neighborhood. Two quick lefts and I was turning into my driveway. I threw my computer bag and my pocketbook over my shoulder and got out of the car. I stepped onto the front stoop and shakingly put the key in the lock. Suddenly, the front door opened for me, and my daughter greeted me crying. "I'm sorry, Mom. Nothing broke. I'm all right," she cried. And there on the floor of the living room was the Christmas tree, ornaments all over the living room rug just as it had been shown to me. My mouth was agape. I was in shock.

"Don't be mad, Mom," my daughter cried, "I'm sorry."

I couldn't speak. All I could do was hug her, be relieved she was all right, and feel gratitude for my connection with Spirit and the Universe. It was through this evidence that they shared with me that knew they were communicating with me.

That was thirty-three years ago and from that moment on, I have looked at my clairs differently. The thoughts that pop into my head are not my wild imagination. I know them to be magical messages from Spirit or my guides. I pay attention to them all—never dismissing them, always trying to understand the message in them that is meant for me. I have trained myself to see signs and coincidences differently. I have trained myself to listen and I have learned to trust my intuition undeniably. When there is a question about clarity, I look for the evidence, or I ask for the evidence, and it is always given to me.

Sometimes, the messages come to comfort me or to let me know people on the other side are around me and supporting me, like when I smell my husband's cigarettes in my new home that no one has ever smoked in. Sometimes the messages give me insights, hints, or ideas into the answers I seek. Sometimes the messages make me laugh, like the time my car windows kept going up and down when it was pouring rain. Sometimes the messages warn me, like they did when the Christmas tree fell on my daughter.

I constantly think of the words, "Ask and you shall receive," and know this to be true. Spirit and the Universe are continually listening, watching, communicating with, and guiding us all. If you are not sure of a divine message's meaning, ask for evidence. Cultivate your connection, be open to it, and always be grateful for the magic it brings into your life.

Reflection

Do you receive divine messages, signs, or synchronicities in your life?

How do you tell the difference between random thoughts and divine messages?

What evidence have you received that allowed you to trust your intuition?

Uncovering Gems on a Career Path

FELICIA MESSINA-D'HAITI

Has there ever been something that you've done that you are completely uninterested in and found that it changed your life? During my freshman year in high school, my parents signed me up for a spring break trip to visit Italy and Switzerland. At that time, I didn't even know what it meant to visit another country. My dad wanted me to visit my "roots" and told me how his parents would have paid for him to visit Italy, but at that time, he was making a significant career change and declined to go. Once there, I was fascinated with everything I saw and had lots of fun. We visited Rome, Vatican City, Florence, Venice, Italy, and Geneva, Switzerland. That short trip was terrific, yet I still did not know how it would create ripples in my future choices, primarily related to my education and career.

Since I was a child, I had wanted to be a nurse like my grandmother, after whom I was named. (I'm actually named after two nurses in our family, my grandmother and my cousin.) I thought nursing was part of my destiny. Later, in middle school, my dad talked to me about my career choices and said if I wanted to go into the medical field, why not be a doctor? So, after some thought, I shifted my aspirations to becoming a pediatrician. I took all the math and science classes I could in high school. I squeezed more than five years' worth of science and math classes into my four years in high school.

The summer before my senior year, I received a call from my school's assistant principal, informing me that my requested schedule had a conflict. Two of the science classes I wanted to take coincided. She placed me in the chemistry class because the other class, human physiology, required chemistry as a prerequisite or to be taken concurrently. In addition, to fill in the extra class period, she had a proposal for me. There was a new class offered that year, filled with mostly seniors, but she thought it would be an excellent class for me to take. The name of the class was "Humanities." I felt disappointed. Not only was I missing out on human physiology, I had no idea what this "Humanities" was—nor was I interested in taking it. But I didn't feel I had much choice, so I reluctantly agreed.

On the first day of class, we were greeted by a tall, elegant woman wearing a long, flowy skirt who described her goals for the class: she would transform us into sophisticated and cultured young ladies. That year, we explored art, music, dance, and other performing arts throughout history. We also visited museums and attended plays, concerts, and the ballet. This class opened an entirely new world I had no idea existed, but it reminded me of that trip to Italy and Switzerland and the art I saw there. I loved this class so much that I tried to fit it into my schedule the following year, as well as an independent study. It didn't work out, but I still attended several field trips and the annual New York City trip to visit museums and see *Les Misérables*.

When it came time to apply to colleges, I was still focused on applying to pre-med programs. Yet, during my senior year, I began to explore options for what it might look like to study art history and pre-medicine. Once I saw that it was possible to do both, I maintained that I wanted to be a doctor and moved forward with that original plan. During my first semester in college, I remember sitting in a botany class, wondering why I had to sit through botany class with one hundred other students looking at the lines in the leaves. The class was boring and didn't seem related to anything that would help me later in life (I now know how it relates, but that's a different story).

I began to ask questions of different advisors I was associated with about selecting a major in the Art History Department. I didn't expect to be met with such fierce resistance. I was given lectures about there not being enough women minorities in the medical field, about not being able to make a living with an art history major, and more. Instead of deterring me, their words pushed me to do more research. I met with an art history graduate who worked in an art gallery, and I began looking for summer internships in the museum field. That summer, I worked in the Prints and Photographs Division of the Library of Congress and had a wonderful experience cataloging artworks.

Then, as my junior year approached, I returned to Italy to study art history for a year. This year was amazing: viewing artworks in their original locations, deeply diving into Italian culture, meeting relatives in Sicily, and traveling around Europe and Egypt. During this year, I received insights into the power of environments and of seeing artwork in the intended locations of their artists. In spending time with a classmate in Cairo, I first learned how to meditate. Living in Italy, I also felt a sense of familiarity, partly because I'd visited before but also because I was connected through my paternal ancestors.

Later, when I discussed my shift from the medical field to art history, my dad commented that he never thought I would attend medical school because he saw my passions elsewhere. Stepping into museum work was a joy. I worked at several museums in New York, New Jersey, and Washington, DC. My favorite department to work in was the education department. As a child of two educators who swore she would never be a teacher, teaching called to me. Throughout the rest of my undergraduate career and graduate art history and museum studies, I gravitated toward museum education roles, which evolved into teaching art history and creating museum-style exhibitions in a public middle school.

After about ten years of working in public education, teaching art and art history, and then coaching teachers, I searched for missing puzzle pieces in my work. After some exploration and attending a women's retreat, I received an assignment to make a list of all the things that I'm passionate about. The exploration of this list, which included art history, color, interior design, photography, teaching, yoga, meditation, and more, could all be drawn together into one major theme. They all related to the study of environments and the many different ways we can shift the energy in our environments.

And while all these interests may seem random and unrelated, I can now reflect on that first trip to Italy. I see how I connected to the love of ancient buildings and art, seeing them in public areas and throughout cities (not just in museums), and how that helped to shape how I view spaces. My work with students, seeing their artwork in our museum exhibits and in real museums, demonstrated to me the importance of seeing ourselves in our spaces. I see how that led to my first experiences with meditation and immersing myself in different cultures. I still see where I work in a healing industry but from a different perspective of arranging environments to create sacred spaces. It taught me to be open to new experiences and to surrender to things looking differently than I imagined because we never really know what anything is for as we move along the journey.

Reflection

When in your life did you feel you "knew" your path, only to discover something more aligned with your talents and dreams? What did you do to honor that nudge?

In what ways are you open to new experiences? In what ways are you not open to them?

How have your parents/caregivers influenced your decisions? What happened when you disagreed with their recommendations?

Divine Peace

WIOLETA KAPUSTA

I had no idea that my desperate call for God's help would launch a journey to discover my soul's purpose.

After I'd earned my MBA, I realized that the corporate life no longer worked for me. I earned my real estate license and dove headfirst into multiple listings, serving my clients to find the homes of their dreams. I loved every moment of that experience—until I didn't. What had given me joy, resulted instead in inner turmoil and dissatisfaction. Clients grew more challenging. I felt frustrated, confused, and annoyed—all the time and with everyone.

I knew that I ought to be grateful for the abundance of opportunities that came my way. I also knew that the tension and constant stress weren't healthy for me. The push-and-pull of these conflicting beliefs threatened to upend my marriage, disrupted my ability to serve my clients, and impacted my mental health.

Until one day. I sat on the brown, leather couch in my living room, resting and becoming present with my turbulent feelings. Suddenly, I stood and, as if drawn there by a magnetic force, placed my hands the back of one of my dining room chairs. Raising my eyes to the heavens, I said, "God, help me here. Give me a clear sign for what I ought to do next."

Immediately, I felt a sense of relief, knowing that I'd placed my order with the Divine and trusting that the answers would come to me. All I had to do was remain attentive and notice any signs that came before me.

As it turned out, I'd registered for an event run by a former real estate agent who was close to my age. I felt a certain kinship with her, especially after having attended a previous event run by her. The event would help me hone my community-building skills by hosting a summit. I hoped these skills would enhance my real estate career and help me bring in steadier income.

The event dates approached on the heels of my cries for help. I pushed aside all my negative feelings and focused on the anticipation of reconnecting with the amazing people I'd met before. I secretly hoped as well for new connections. I reveled in the fact that I'd just sold three houses, and my commissions paid for the program.

The venue was packed. People pushed their way through corridors towards sessions, bumping into each other in their hurry. I was no different. As I scurried from one classroom to the next, I slammed into a woman named Carrie. When I saw who it was, I chuckled a little. We'd run into each other before—literally. The first meeting felt like a coincidence. The second time got my full attention. Carrie and I smiled at each other.

"We have to stop meeting like this," I said, as we compared schedules.

Realizing the jam-packed sessions left little time for more conversation, we exchanged contact information, agreeing to reconnect later that day. I walked away, noticing that I felt strangely calm and peaceful.

Those same feelings showed up when Carrie and I sat down for our chat.

Carrie said, "I set an intention before coming here that I would attract the perfect woman to attend my retreat." She went on to say that her luxury retreat immediately followed the ZONE event. "Would you like to join us?"

I had some thinking to do. Not only was there a significant cash outlay required, I would also need to extend my trip and I wasn't sure that was possible. "I'll discuss this with my husband and see if I can make it work." I agreed to give Carrie an answer the following day.

I felt nervous about approaching my husband. Our relationship wasn't on solid footing and his patience with me in short supply. I called him and explained what I hoped to do. "I know I need this. For me. For us," I said. Begrudgingly, he agreed. I still felt conflicted.

I fortunately shared accommodations with my friend Katori. During our time together at the ZONE event, we comfortably shared deeply and vulnerably. She listened to me patiently, offering insight and support.

During one of our talks, Katori said, "Put one of your hands on your heart and the other on your belly. Breathe. Be present. What do you need?"

I barely slept that night as I wavered between placating my husband or attending the retreat. In the morning, I decided to say "yes" and rearranged my schedule, all the while the little voice inside my head questioned the retreat cost. Money didn't come easily to me and there was a part of me that struggled to invest in myself. *I'll trade my peace of mind for peace of heart.*

During the retreat and for a year afterward, I worked with Carrie. I healed, transforming my heart and mind. I saw things in a new light, felt more peaceful, and reveled in joy and love. Additional divine synchronicities appeared to more I followed my intuition and aligned with my inner self.

With each step, I opened like a lotus to the sun, receiving and accepting guidance on my next steps. I no longer sought fulfillment externally but found instead a home within myself. As I leaned into this transformative experience, challenges appeared testing my willingness to grow. I soon realized that I no longer wanted to solely help people find their physical homes, I wanted to invite them into the spirit realm of their inner homes.

Every day, I feel blessed and grateful to be on this journey. Answering my divine calling deepened my relationships with God, my husband, my daughter, and others in my life. Most importantly, it deepened my trust in myself. How divine!

Reflection

What inner turmoil do you get to address to find peace in your heart?

What does it mean to you to find your inner home?

What could your life look like when you choose to follow your divine call?

The Labyrinth

CRYSTAL COCKERHAM

"That again?" The answer was a swift and definitive, "Yes." It was another layer of healing that needed to happen and wow, this stung at my core.

I take time off between December and January for sacred family time. I also spend time in reflection, clearing, envisioning, and planning, both personally and professionally. This past year, the reflection was deep. When this surfaced again, it surprised me.

I dropped into the process of working through this layer and the feeling of deep betrayal and deep hurt. I know now that these unprocessed feelings led to subconscious self-sabotage. I had had incredible momentum and was feeling spiritually, emotionally, and physically successful until my website disappeared for nearly two months in early 2021. At the time, I felt like someone had kidnapped my baby, ripped a part of me away.

To make it worse, I found out the day after I'd dashed up north because my dad had been rushed to the hospital after being trapped on the floor for three days due to a series of strokes. Oh, and did I happen to mention it was early 2021, and there was a pandemic in progress? So he wasn't allowed a visitor to advocate for him in addition to everything else the pandemic affected.

To say it felt like my world was spinning out of control is an understatement. I found myself utilizing every coping tool I had learned over the years: breath work, meditation, prayer, moving energy, journaling, and more.

Six weeks later, and numerous hours of phone conversations and extra money spent, an outdated version of my website was recovered. She wasn't the same. I wasn't the same. It took being hit by a cosmic two-by-four with a tsunami force, but a rebranding I'd known for some time was needed began with a new website.

Meanwhile, it was the North American supermoon solar eclipse. I didn't have the special viewing gear, but a lovely group of ladies offered me an extra pair. I knew I needed to be outside in the energies so I could release and receive guidance around my business. I chose a place near me with a labyrinth that I very much enjoy frequenting.

As I sat on the bench in the beautiful gardens reflecting, I opened my journal and began writing:

"I feel like the past few years have been a series of failed starts. This past year, I have felt stuck and found myself clearing more energy from early 2021 and the rebrand. I find myself questioning what I am doing—why am I still trying through the exhaustion of everything: personal loss of family members, my own personal health challenges, and the severe dip in business movement? I choose to release the hide-in-the-corner-because-someone-deeply-hurt-me-and-derailed-my-business mode. I came here to shine my light, not to hide, point, and shoot light arrows out of defense and live in survival mode ... I had been giving and giving and giving—over-delivering with little progress, and, at times, none. As I reflect on this, I suppose the deep, unhealed hurt is what made me pull back on how I was showing up for myself in my business. Yet, as I write this, I find myself asking: Is it worth it? Does anyone really care? Do I care? Do I keep on trying?"

Yes, that last bit really caught me by surprise. The labyrinth was finally free; it was my turn to walk it. Afterwards, I returned to the bench where I'd watched the eclipse, opened my journal back up, and recorded my experience with a lump still in my throat and tears streaming down my face. This was my experience as recorded in my journal:

"I just finished walking the labyrinth. I felt an incredible sensation about three-quarters of the way out, when suddenly I felt the left side of my body lighten so quickly, I felt dizzy and disoriented as if the earth disappeared beneath me. I paused. Gasped. Put my hands over my heart, tears welling up, angel bumps all over, and said, 'Thank you.' I took another moment to connect with my breath and ground before finishing my outbound tour.

Once completed, I again gave gratitude and followed my soul's guidance back to the spot where I first felt the incredible sensation on the left side of my body … Again, I stood there so I could try to process this magical moment. [Make no mistake about it. This was absolutely magical, miraculous even.]

My body was shaking from the vibrational shift, from the release of what I had been carrying. Tears were flowing; I had a lump in my throat, yet I wasn't crying. I was about to ask my spiritual allies who or what had gifted me that experience when I saw angel wings in my minds' eye and knew I had just been touched by an angel."

Was the knowing that easy? Yes! It was absolutely and undeniably an angelic encounter. The knowing was accompanied by a visceral confirmation of what I refer to as angel bumps—when it feels like every hair on my body is standing up with an amplified chill, accompanied by a flooding of energy up and down my spine.

As I wrote, I became clearer. Of course, those questions had to come up! The me who was hurt had to ask the questions I didn't have time for when my website disappeared, and I was helping my dad through months of recovery. It was time to step up and walk myself through the process of healing and transforming the hurt.

It's time to redefine and refine what my business looks like, again. Only this time it's going to be absolutely, magically, fantabulous because this time, I am doing so by standing in my power, driven by my passion and purpose, not from the defensive I-don't-want-to-lose-what-I-have-worked-so-hard-for energy, while trying to hold everything together.

The Divine has my back and I know it, because I felt it.

Nearly a month passed before I shared my experience with a dear friend of mine, who is an exceptional spiritual healer and medium. When I shared my story with her, I reached about the midway point when she too was flooded with angel bumps. I paused. Her eyes were in full-on channel mode, and she asked me, "Who gave you the rose?"

Once more, I felt a shift, as if I was floating. Before I could answer, she asked another question, "Which divine feminine figure have you been calling upon?" I gasped, my heart jumped, and with a lump in my throat I replied, "Mother Mary."

No longer in channeling mode, both of us sharing the charged energetics of paused time and being energetically wide open, she looked at me and said, "Holy shit, Crystal! Mother Mary and Archangel ____ at the same time!?"

I was in awe all over again as I replied, "Yes," though I hadn't realized or acknowledged Mother Mary until this moment. I was aware of how blessed my experience was, I just wasn't aware of the double blessing it was!

It made perfect sense though. The month of March brought on countless Hail Marys when I found out one of my aunts was in transition, the cancer overcoming her will, and with the birth of my first grandchild. What I didn't know, what I didn't realize, was that I too needed Mother Mary's grace, compassion and blessing.

Reflecting back, I had to share this with my dear friend, whose name just so happens to be Rose Marie, so I could acknowledge, accept, and process the enormity of this magical and miraculous divine synchronicity. Together, Mother Mary and the Archangel, who I am choosing to leave unnamed, relieved me of both the burden and the wound, along with healing my body where I had been carrying it.

The angel bumps have always been divine confirmation for me, my soul's way of affirming a divine synchronicity. There's magic in the moment when everything, including time, seems to stand still, where you can see and feel the energies around you as if the air is electrically charged. There's no denying, this was one of those moments for me.

Reflection

How have angels and archangels guided you on your life's journey?

What time of the year do you set aside for sacred connection and reflection? What's your process like during this time?

Write about a time where a loved one was undergoing something, and you knew it energetically. What was that experience like and how has it impacted you since?

Serendipity and the Path to Mindful Gratitude

JUDY GALLAURESI

I have had my fair share of anxiety and stress over the years. Regrets about the past and paralyzing fear about the future. At times, I have felt as though I was drowning and couldn't catch my breath. My thoughts often spiral out of control, leaving me feeling helpless and overwhelmed.

My mindfulness journey began as a young woman in the spring of 1982. My internist and gynecologist (both men) pooh-poohed my debilitating headaches and chest pain and blamed all my issues on hormones or anxiety. They were both hell-bent on prescribing Valium, which they said would take care of everything. I knew in my gut that was not the answer. After many months of prodding my internist, he relented and scheduled tests.

I was twenty-one years old, rode horses, was in school and working part-time, and had stars in my eyes about my next big adventure. How does living daily in this much pain happen to someone my age? I came to realize that stress, living on caffeine and nicotine, lack of sleep, and not dealing with growing up in a very volatile family had taken its toll.

On a damp, chilly spring day in 1982, I jumped out of my car in a parking garage. I was going to have a smoke and finish my coffee there, but the stench of car fumes, rotting trash, and urine nauseated me. I dashed down the stairs to get fresh air. Looking back, I wonder what I was thinking. Fresh air? I was smoking like a chimney. Looking at my watch, I saw I was late.

I was harried as I got on the elevator, not noticing I had pressed the wrong floor. As I hastily exited, I nearly knocked over a doctor. I apologized and blurted out, "I'm so sorry. I've been told my entire life I should watch where I'm going and not be such a scatterbrain." Before I could even ask for the quickest route to radiology, he said to take a deep breath and then asked where I needed to be.

He was one of the kindest people I had met in a very long time, and so peaceful I thought he was a figment of my imagination. He offered to walk me to the radiology department and led me through a maze of hallways. Little did I know that this man, Jon Kabat-Zin, would put me on a path of mindfulness. I had no idea he was coaching me with what would become his signature MBSR system as we walked.

All I knew was that I felt calm for the first time in years. I thanked him profusely and said, "I don't know what kind of voodoo you do, but this is the best I've felt in years."

The elephant sitting on my chest was gone. My headache was not a pounding stampede of horses but a dull ache. He handed me his card and said, "When you're ready and have your test results, call my office. I can help you." I deliberated for more than six months about whether to see him.

When I mentioned it to friends and family, they asked, "Why do you think you need a shrink?" I had no idea what kind of doctor he was. His card just said PhD. What I did know was that I didn't want to live that way anymore, taking whatever prescriptions the doctors threw at me and feeling miserable. I believe Jon Kabat-Zinn was put in front of me that day by Divine Spirit to intervene and show me a better way to live.

So, in late 1982, I embarked on a journey to find inner peace and contentment. That quest led to a basement room at the hospital and to the practice of mindfulness—a word not heard very much in those days. By focusing on my breath and the sensations in my body, I learned to observe my thoughts without judgment. This simple act transformed my life, fully allowing me to experience and appreciate BE-ing present.

Every time I entered the softly lit hallway and heard my footsteps echoing as I walked to the clinic, the sound was a meditative drumbeat, a healing salve to my heart and soul. To this day, hearing my footsteps echoing as I walk is soothing. Those weekly visits changed my life in ways I couldn't have imagined back then.

Along my journey, I discovered the incredible power of gratitude. Embracing gratitude became a cornerstone of my existence, an anchor in the tumultuous sea of life. Each morning and evening, I dedicated time to reflect on what I was thankful for, whether small or insignificant. This practice of acknowledging gratitude wasn't just a routine; it was a lifeline. It shifted my perspective, illuminating the beauty in the mundane and the extraordinary in the everyday. The ritual of cataloging my gratitudes began with the simplest of pleasures. The sight of the night sky, a tapestry of twinkling stars in the serene silence of the night, was a reminder of the vastness of the universe and the fleeting nature of my troubles.

These moments under the celestial dome gave me a profound peace, a stark contrast to the cacophony of sirens and the constant rumble of trucks that characterized my work reality as a military analyst. Holding a hot cup of tea became a meditative act, the warmth seeping into my cold hands as I braced myself for the uncertainties of my next assignment. This small comfort was a beacon of hope, a momentary respite from the literal and metaphorical cold I faced in my work.

This gratitude extended beyond the physical to the emotional and mental strengths I was building. I became grateful for the resilience that mindfulness and gratitude instilled in me. The ability to find a sliver of joy or a moment of peace amidst chaos was like discovering a vein of gold in the rock. My evening reflections often included gratitude for the day's challenges because each taught me more about my strength, ability to adapt, and the depth of my resolve.

Through mindfulness, I learned to ride the waves of life with grace, but gratitude taught me to see the beauty in the ebb and flow itself. This dual practice became my lifeline, transforming moments of quiet reflection and every interaction and experience throughout my day. Whether it was the warmth of a smile from a stranger, the laughter of children playing, or the serene silence that followed a snowfall, my heart grew in its capacity to hold joy for these ordinary, everyday miracles. These simple blessings took me away from the chaos of my personal and professional life.

My life choices and career have taken me to many interesting places and tenuous situations. Being grateful, centered, and present in the moment isn't about ignoring or disconnecting from the world. Instead, it means fully engaging in life—the good, the bad, and the ugly—while maintaining balance and inner calm. I realized that much like riding my horse, I hold the reins of my life, and my thoughts can shape my reality. My choice every day is mindful living.

Mindfulness and gratitude reshaped my narrative from one of surviving to one of thriving. There is something to be thankful for in every moment, and in finding it, I shifted my focus from what I lacked to the abundance in my life. This shift was not just mental; it manifested in my physical world, improving relationships, opening doors to new opportunities, and deepening my connection to the world around me.

Right now, I'm living the most rewarding adventure of my life, immersed in a journey teeming with growth, healing, and a continuously deepening love for the here and now. My daily devotion to mindfulness and gratitude isn't just routine; it's the solid ground I walk on. Armed with a heart brimming with gratitude and a soul eager to welcome what comes next, I stand ready. Life's twists and turns? Bring them on. I'm here for it all, with open arms and a spirit ready to soar on this serendipitous path of mindful gratitude.

Reflection

Who has shown up in your life and changed it so completely that who you were afterward was different than who you had been? What would you say to that person?

How has gratitude shifted your belief in yourself and your lived experience?

Where have resilience and grace shown up in your life? How does recognizing them affect you now?

From Crossroads to Clarity: Discovering Divine Guidance

SHARON SEABERG

"Allow your passion to become your purpose, and it will one day become your profession." Gabby Bernstein's words echoed in my soul as I reflected on a pivotal moment in my life—a moment that beckoned me toward transformation. It began with a difficult conversation, a dreaded reorganization at work, and a daunting future reporting to someone I found challenging. Little did I know that was the universe nudging me towards a path filled with divine synchronicities.

"I can't do this. You have to find something else for me," I told my boss, my voice a mixture of fear and frankness. I had a great relationship with him and thought I could be honest with him. He had just broken the news of the reorganization. I was to report to a woman known for taking credit for others' work, including mine. At that point, I was successful yet deeply unhappy, respected, yet burnt out. My job demanded constant overtime and travel, leaving me exhausted and disconnected from my family and friends. I had clues about my burnout, such as difficulty finding words and itchy skin, but I had been overriding these hints.

The woman who would soon be my boss had a reputation that preceded her. At a sales conference at the Mirage in Las Vegas, she presented a marketing strategy I had developed as if it were her own. When confronted, she dismissively said she didn't think I could handle it alone. That kind of undermining eroded my enthusiasm for a job I once loved.

The universe often speaks in whispers, but sometimes it roars. Before the Christmas break, my boss had delivered the news that there would be a reorganization, and he had responded that there was nothing that he could do about the changes. I spent the holidays wrapped in a blanket of worry. When we returned to the office, I noticed he canceled our calls. I figured he was ignoring me since he could not give me what I wanted. When we finally met, he delivered news that would shake the very foundations of my world: my position was being eliminated. What shocked me was how I felt about it. I had an overwhelming sense of relief! Don't get me wrong. I had all the feelings about it…anger, fear, dread, sadness, but the overriding feeling was relief. It was as if a weight was lifted, signaling that perhaps this end was just a new beginning.

Armed with a severance package and a heart full of uncertainty, I stepped into the unknown. This period of transition was a gift in disguise. It allowed me to reconnect with myself—to discover what truly mattered. During this time, I began to notice the first threads of divine synchronicity begin to weave their magic into my life, leading me to unexplored paths and unexpected opportunities.

In the quiet of those first weeks, I untangled years of accumulated stress and rediscover passions long buried under corporate responsibilities. I found solace in long walks, the pages of inspiring books, and the comforting chaos of my daughters' laughter. This time also allowed me to reconnect with my husband, who had been my steadfast support through the ups and downs of my career.

Divine Synchronicity

Almost effortlessly, a new job opportunity landed in my lap. I didn't have to send out a ton of resumes or do a ton of interviews. I was invited to join this new company, and the similarities to my last job were crazy. The role was remote, had similar pay, and my new boss even looked like the woman who would have been my boss at my previous company. This role was not just another job; it was a sign. My new company invited me to a sales kickoff at none other than the Mirage in Las Vegas—the same place where the last seeds of my previous life's discontent had been sown. This time, however, I was welcomed with applause and appreciation, starkly contrasting to when I had worked so hard and got no recognition. It was as if the universe showed me that I didn't need to prove my worth; I simply needed to show up and be myself.

This synchronicity was not lost on me. A profound sense of healing enveloped me as I walked into the same conference room where I had once felt so undervalued. It was as if every step I took in that room retraced and repaired the pathways of my self-doubt. The applause from my new colleagues was not just for my presence but seemed to acknowledge my journey and resilience.

When I was in the middle of my burnout, I investigated doing a coaching program for women in burnout. The program I found was costly. I had never spent that much on myself for self-development. During the layoff conversation with my boss, I found myself being brave. I asked if the company would pay for the program. Maybe he felt guilty, but for whatever reason, he said yes.

I jumped headfirst into the program. I discovered that I loved this kind of work. When I finished that program, there was another one calling my name. I let myself go a little overboard with the number of courses I took. Eventually, I realized that I had found my passion.

I discovered becoming a coach was more than just an educational experience; it was a communal journey of awakening. I rediscovered my power and the importance of intuition. The friendships I formed came with an understanding that we were all intertwined in each other's journeys, supporting and elevating one another.

With my new job providing the stability I craved, I ventured into life coaching. Balancing this with my corporate role, I found that the principles of coaching enhanced my leadership and deepened my relationships.

The impact on my family was palpable. My daughters thrived, becoming more confident and engaged in their own lives. My husband and I found a new depth to our relationship, bonded by our shared support of each other's dreams.

Eventually, the call to coach full-time became undeniable. Embracing this path meant leaving behind the security of my corporate life, but the pull of my passion was stronger. I leaped, trusting that the synchronicities that had guided me this far would continue to light my way.

Starting my coaching practice was both thrilling and daunting. Each client brought unique challenges and opportunities for growth—for them and me. As my practice grew, so did my understanding of the transformative power of coaching. I was not just helping others but continuously learning and evolving myself.

Reflecting on my journey, I see a tapestry woven with threads of challenge, change, and chance. Losing my job wasn't just an ending but a profound redirection. This journey taught me that life's divine synchronicities are not mere coincidences; they are signposts guiding us toward our true paths, urging us to trust in the unfolding of our destinies.

Life is truly about the journey—the unfolding magic, the moments of wonder, and the incredible people we meet along the way. It's not about rushing to a destination but about savoring the experiences that fill our days, teaching and shaping us into who we are meant to be. The best part of this journey is our unpredictable and awe-inspiring path, where every encounter and challenge holds a spark of the divine waiting to be discovered. These elements—the laughter shared with a stranger, the awe of a breathtaking sunset, the wisdom gained from a difficult day—are not just steps along a path but are the essence of a richly lived life. Embrace this adventure with open arms and an open heart, for the beauty of life lies in these very journeys, woven together by the magic and wonder of everyday experiences.

This journey taught me to open my heart to the universe's whispers. Embrace the synchronicities that beckon me to follow. Trust in the magic of beginnings masquerading as endings, and know that each step forward is a step toward a life filled with purpose and joy. Let us walk this path together, embracing the divine synchronicities that promise to transform our lives miraculously. And trust in the process, knowing that the universe has a way of guiding you, even through the detours.

Reflection

What are the divine synchronicities that have appeared in your life, and how have they guided you toward your dreams?

When have you felt the most supported by the universe, and how did those moments change your perspective or decisions?

What are the lessons you've learned from the challenges you've faced, and how have they prepared you for future opportunities?

CHAPTER TWO

Soul Nudges to Reclaimed Health

Navigating Life's Challenges with Resilience

BRENDA REIMER-HARDER

From my twenties to my late forties, amid a seemingly picture-perfect life, I was drowning in disillusionment. Despite a loving family and career success, I felt trapped in a cycle of abuse and dysfunction. Patterns emerged in my relationships, where initial bliss soured into emotional neglect and manipulation. I struggled to reconcile this reality with the dream of the marriage and family I'd envisioned.

As time went by and amid the seemingly idyllic life of motherhood and career success, I found myself suffocating, engulfed in the emotional turmoil and depression that followed. My life appeared picture-perfect, with a loving family and a successful career, yet beneath it all lay a tangled web of dysfunction and unfulfillment. The cracks in my seemingly perfect world widened, revealing a reality far removed from the dreams I once held within my heart.

I grappled with questions of self-worth and fulfillment, haunted by past traumas and toxic relationships. Reflecting on my past, I realized recurring themes of disruption and resilience. From childhood instability to tumultuous relationships, I carried emotional wounds that manifested as physical and psychological ailments.

The mental and emotional backlash manifested as headaches, chronic fatigue, and fibromyalgia. Yet, amidst the chaos, clarity emerged, guiding me toward healing.

Seeking solace, I embarked on a journey of self-discovery, embracing holistic practices and spiritual teachings. Through therapy and group counseling, I confronted past traumas and reclaimed my sense of self-worth. I learned to view my struggles not as setbacks but as opportunities for growth.

It was a profound realization, akin to the earth cracking beneath my feet. I questioned how I had arrived at that juncture, feeling emotionally battered and drained despite outward success and my polished appearance. The trajectory of my relationships mirrored a tragic arc, beginning with euphoria only to descend into emotional neglect and abuse. I grappled with the clash between the idealized notion of marriage and family and the stark reality of my own experience.

Leaving behind yet another toxic relationship was both liberating and daunting—a leap of faith into the unknown. Yet, with each step forward, I felt the weight of expectation and societal norms lift. Surrounded by supportive friends and mentors, I embarked on a journey of self-realization, reclaiming empowerment over my life and destiny.

Reflecting on my journey as a youth, I discerned a recurring pattern of disturbance and resilience from a tumultuous childhood marked by addictions, incestual dysfunction, and instability to unrestrained relationships fraught with confusion. I carried the scars of my past like invisible wounds. The brokenness inside manifested as psychological and physical conditions, weighing heavily on my spirit and stifling my sense of self-worth. Yet, amidst the chaos, glimmers of clarity emerged, guiding me toward healing and self-discovery.

Looking back on my foulest relationships, I recognized patterns of disruption and drama, marked by initial bliss followed by disillusionment and betrayal, as a devoted young mother and partner to these controlling and insecure men. I shouldered the burden of household responsibilities and emotional labor, feeling trapped in a role that stifled my authenticity. These experiences led me to a passage towards safety and survival.

Throughout my life, I moved from one living situation to another, seeking security and peace but often finding myself discontented and stripped of my dignity and power. Despite the challenges, my unwavering commitment to freedom and self-expression kept me from settling for less than I deserved.

In my quest for love and acceptance, I settled for partners who couldn't meet my emotional needs, including a few relationships with narcissists that left me feeling trapped and unfulfilled. Despite the hardships, my love for my children gave me strength and purpose, inspiring me to seek healing and transformation.

Further, to having an unplanned child at sixteen, and twelve years later, giving birth to one and then a year and a half later beautiful healthy daughters, and acquiring a stepson I adore. While I consider them blessings, it was challenging to share the responsibility with their fathers, who saw me as their rival, but I loved our kids and did the best I knew how for them then. It was a tumultuous endeavor, shaping the lives of our sons and daughters, but all in all, I am grateful and so proud of who they are now and who they are becoming.

Holistic and alternative practices became my refuge amidst the struggles. Despite the challenges, I found solace in nurturing my children and pursuing my career. Self-care rituals, like reading, writing, parenting and self-help classes, and gym memberships, became anchors amidst life's storms.

Seeking support and guidance, I turned to self-help books, therapy, and holistic practices, confronting past traumas and reclaiming my sense of self. Through group counseling and self-reflection, I gained insights into the patterns of abuse and dysfunction that had shaped my life. Through introspection and journaling, I set intentions for my desired life, cultivating a vision of abundance and joy.

As I embarked on a journey of self-discovery, I began to recognize the link between emotional turmoil and physical illness. Despite diagnoses of depression, chronic fatigue, and fibromyalgia, I refused to let these conditions define me, seeking holistic alternatives for healing and growth.

My path to healing led me to explore spiritual teachings and alternative therapies, including energy healing, psychic, intuitive counseling, Oracle and Tarot card readings, and mindfulness practices using journalling and law of attraction techniques. Through these practices, I tapped into my intuition and reclaimed my power, learning to trust the universe's wisdom.

Through these practices, I learned to cultivate inner peace and resilience, anchoring myself amidst life's storms and preparing myself for who and what I would become.

Leaving behind a toxic marriage marked by manipulation and dysfunction, I found the courage to pursue a new life on my own terms. Embracing the principles of self-love and acceptance, I joined support groups and sought out like-minded individuals who supported my journey.

Through manifestation and intention-setting, I began to envision the life I desired, cultivating a sense of abundance and gratitude. With each step forward, I let go of the past and embraced the possibilities of the present moment and future.

Finding love again, I entered a new partnership built on mutual respect and understanding. Together, we love traveling, dancing, golfing, and enjoying a life that was more than I imagined. We moved in and out of a few homes filled with love, peace, friends, and family connections--manifesting the vision I had held in my heart for so long.

It has been a journey marked by synchronicity—serendipitous

encounters and fortuitous twists of fate that seemed to guide me along my path—from chance meetings to unexpected opportunities, each synchronistic moment served as a signpost, affirming that I was on the right track. The universe conspired to lead me toward a life of authenticity and fulfillment.

As I look back on my journey, I am filled with gratitude for the synchronicities and blessings that have guided me along the way. Through the trials and tribulations, I have emerged stronger and more resilient, ready to embrace the wonder of life's journey.

With each twist and turn, I discovered the power of resilience and the beauty of life's synchronicities. Today, I stand empowered, grateful for the lessons learned and the community that uplifts me. I find peace and gratitude in embracing the journey, knowing that life's wonders await everywhere.

Leaving behind the pain of the past, I embarked on a journey of self-discovery, determined to carve out a life of joy and fulfillment. Surrounded by a community of kindred spirits, I found the courage to speak my truth and live authentically unapologetically.

As I opened myself up to the possibilities of the universe, I was met with synchronicities and blessings that reaffirmed my faith in the divine. With each twist and turn of the road, I found myself guided by an unseen hand, leading me toward a destiny filled with love and abundance.

Today, as I look back on my journey, I am filled with gratitude for every obstacle and challenge that has crossed my path, for it is through adversity that we discover our strength and through the darkness that we find the light within us.

With an open heart and a spirit of resilience, I embrace the wonders of life's journey, knowing that every step has brought me closer to my truest self. Namaste!

Reflection

How would you change the narrative and characters if you could live your life over?

If you could change your life's trajectory, what type of life would you wish for?

If you could make a difference in other people's lives, who would you choose to help?

The Bear Story

SARA GOMEZ

I saw the number as I picked up my cell phone. My stomach dropped. I took a quick, shallow inhale, "Hello?"

Silence. Then, a deep sigh. I already knew. "Sara, I'm so sorry." The voice on the other end trailed off into the distance.

I don't remember ending the call. The pain ripped through my body like a wildfire. My knees buckled, gave way, and my bottom smacked onto the cold bathroom tile. A guttural wail came from deep within. My teacup poodle, Oliver, scurried into my lap, licking my tears away. I called my husband at work but couldn't get words out through the sobs.

"I'm on my way home," his voice steady with strength.

We had been down this road. Too many times to count. The numbers tell their own story. Seven years together. Six years of an all-consuming infertility journey. Four failed intrauterine inseminations (IUI). Six failed in-vitro fertilizations (IVF). One excruciating miscarriage. Each time I received that call and heard that sigh, the excitement grew harder and harder to muster, and our hope ripped away once again. The baby things we'd collected went back into the attic. The hands of the clock ticking out of time became deafening—the rage on the other side of despair.

With one embryo left, preparing for my final IVF round, I snuggled into my favorite emerald green couch in my room to meditate. A familiar voice, the one I call my Inner Counselor, whispered, "Go back to the bear story." Curious, I complied, and off I went into the recesses of my memories.

My nine-year-old self, curly hair wild, dressed in ill-fitted hand-me-downs and threadbare sneakers, solemnly schlepped down the hall of our elementary school. Four years earlier, my family had relocated from a hippie commune in Tennessee to a pocket-sized, conservative town in Texas' Bible belt. It was the 1980s, and my rag-tag hippie family rolling into that town was a first as if aliens had been dropped from a spaceship; I struggled to fit in.

It was intermural academic competition season in Texas. Finally old enough to try out, my delight quickly turned to dismay. After bombing another try-out for some math-related event, I walked out of a classroom downtrodden (later, I learned math would never be my thing). Not only was I a weirdo with no friends, but I felt stupid, too! The small lump in my throat morphed into a bowling ball as I tried in vain to swallow it while white-hot tears welled up in my eyes.

The girl's bathroom loomed in front of me. Hastening toward my refuge, desperate not to draw attention to my oncoming torrent of tears, I had just reached the bathroom door when I heard my classmate Amy's voice boisterously reciting a story in a classroom nearby. Gripped as though by a magnetic pull, I glided through the classroom door. Amy stood at the front, reading. I made my way to the back of the room, where stapled papers were stacked on a bookshelf. I picked up a set and began to read to myself.

"Hi, Sara!" I turned toward the front of the classroom, where several teachers sat in a row. "Are you trying out for Prose & Poetry?"

"Um, I guess so. What's prooo…um, what's it again?" I asked, confused as to how I ended up in that room.

"Prose & Poetry. You read a story to an audience as though you are the person telling the story. We pick one student to represent us at the competition. When you're ready, you can come to the front."

When my turn to read came, my stomach jolted, sending a wave of nausea into my throat. I inhaled deeply. I looked down at the paper….and again experienced an instant magnetic pull. I leaped into the story as though I had been swept through the door to Narnia.

I portrayed a five-year-old boy who had wild eyes, a strong lisp, and spoke with the intensity of an old western settler narrowly cheating death.

"I wasth pwaying with a thstick in my backyawd, when sthuddenly…!" I exclaimed. My teachers lean forward in their seats. Suddenly, my stick turned into a sword, my swing set into a giant tree. Then, my whole yard transformed before my eyes into a densely forested mountaintop. I turned towards my house and froze at what stood before me—a growling, snarling Grizzly bear pounding its paws. The thought hit me: I had to save my mom, dad, and baby brother, who were safely inside our home, from this baleful beast. I was the bear slayer! As I recounted the harrowing tale of my brave battle to victory, I noticed, to my amazement, my teachers' eyes bright with childlike wonder, chins resting on palms, hanging onto my every word. They were entranced, and so was I, together on a magical ride of the imagination. I felt free, confident, and utterly amazed that all that had come from me!

Leading up to the competition, there was a buzz in the air. Not only had I been selected to represent Haltings Elementary, but I was also the clear front-runner to secure a gold medal. But as the collective zeal for gold became more palpable, I became more disheartened. It felt like that magical moment in the classroom was taken from me and turned into nothing more than bragging rights and an ornament in the school's trophy case. At the competition, the buzz about me and the bear story had made its way to schools in our district, which only deepened my despondence.

On the day of my performance, I was escorted to a stark, white room and took my place in front of the judges' panel. I was halfway through the story when it happened. I looked down at my once-inked pages, and, to my horror, they were blank, as white as the walls in that room.

I stood frozen until, what felt like minutes, though likely only seconds, the words reappeared, and I carried on. But the damage was done. When my name was announced at the medal ceremony, I was awarded fourth place. My chin sunk to my chest; I let my teachers, my school down.

Confused, I opened my eyes and was back on my emerald green couch. "What does the bear story have to do with IVF?"

"What did YOU want?" whispered my Inner Counselor. I paused.

That question had never occurred to me. I only remembered the despair of letting people down. "I wanted to say no," I muttered. "I didn't want to compete. I just wanted to enjoy that magical experience. I didn't think I had a choice. But I wanted to say no."

I felt that magnetic pull again. My body rose from the couch, and before I knew it, I stood before my husband. *Oh, God…what am I saying? Suck the words back in!* But I couldn't stop —one word stumbling over the next in a race past my lips. "I can't do it. My body is telling me no. It crushes me to say this because you can't fight this battle, and I was determined never to give up because you are the one person I would do anything in the world for. You're the last person on earth I want to let down, and I know it's our last chance, and I'm so sorry and…."

"Sara!" My husband interrupted, "Thank God!" Scooping me into a giant bear hug. "I've been hoping you would say this! I don't want my best friend to put her body through this agony anymore. I don't need anything in this life more than I need YOU."

With a sigh of relief that felt a steam engine billowing smoke as it came to a halt, I melted into his arms. I couldn't believe it.

What I'd been most afraid of, claiming what I needed at the risk of letting down someone I love, was what we both wanted all along. Embracing and laughing, feeling more jovial than we had in years, we talked about adoption and plotted the adventures we'd go on since we weren't chained to a never-ending cycle of fertility treatments. I didn't have a baby yet, but I had ME. And I was pregnant with possibility. And magic.

Reflection

When have you suppressed your needs at the risk of hurting the people you love and care about?

What times did you show up for yourself despite your fear of doing so? What did you learn from those experiences?

Who are the people in your life who encourage you to show up for yourself and get your needs met? How do you nurture those relationships? How might you cultivate more relationships like this?

Kintsugi: A Goddess in the Making

TYWANAH EVETTE

A Japanese art called *kintsugi* involves taking a broken bowl and reconnecting the broken bits with gold filling instead of discarding the debris. Not only is the bowl more valuable, but it's also stronger than before. I can relate!

I will never forget the date: March 19, 2022. I like to say it's the day I transitioned because the version of me who felt so desperately starved for love and attention no longer existed.

I had just returned to Atlanta from Washington, DC, after burying my sister's partner. I had only seen my sister cry once before, when my mother transitioned. My sister was so grief-stricken I had to be strong for her, so there was no time for me to process the grief I felt watching her suffer. My sister was not one to show emotion, so watching her grieve the sudden death of her partner of over twenty years was heartbreaking.

When I boarded my flight back to Atlanta, everything in me screamed, "Go home," but I knew doing so would start an argument I couldn't handle. Even against my best friend advising me to go home, I went to my boyfriend's house instead. Trying to make light conversation on the drive to his house, I mentioned how educational Washington, DC, was and suggested that we take his bright and gifted son to visit the sights and museums.

The air in the car turned cold. I knew this shift meant his insecurities had been triggered and knew he would scream at me all night. He was upset that I would dare suggest that we go someplace together that I had been with to my ex-husband. My boyfriend's insecurities had reached an all-time high.

We were at his house when the argument began. I put my cellphone in my robe pocket and voice-recorded everything he said; I needed to know I wasn't "losing my mind," as he had declared many times. After all, he was a fourth-grade teacher. Who would believe me?

While he screamed, I walked away, numb, and climbed into bed, still recording the madness being spewed at me. He followed me, but I refused to speak and went to sleep for a few hours. The following day, the harassment continued until I broke. I took thirty sleeping pills with coffee, followed by vinegar, walked out of the house, and lay down between two trees, planning to sleep forever.

In my delirium, I saw my mother and stepfather standing at the edge of a forest, telling me, "It's not time. You will now know your purpose; other people need you!"

I desperately wanted to stay with them, but my mother pushed me out of the forest and told me she would see me soon. I didn't understand her message then; I fully comprehend it now.

I awoke in the hospital and was transported to a psychiatric hospital for evaluation. Even there, my boyfriend called to argue, knowing the conversations were recorded. When the nurses saw me upset, they extended my hospital stay by three days.

My daughter, who was twenty-four at the time and my emergency contact, insisted I be discharged to my home only. Even at a young age, she knew what was best for me when I couldn't decide. I was trauma-bonded to my boyfriend and didn't recognize his behavior as abusive. He never hit me, and my low self-esteem led me to believe I deserved his treatment

The day after my discharge, my sister called to invite me to move to Washington, DC, and I accepted. Before I moved, I underwent a Rapid Transformational Therapy (RTT) hypnotherapy session where my mother came through clearly, transferring her psychic gifts to me. She told me she would fiercely protect me.

Despite my fragile emotional state, I moved to DC to help my sister, as well as her six-month-old cane Corso puppy, who also lost "his person." Despite not having yet accepted my psychic gifts, I saw my sister's partner around the house. The dog also noticed him. One day, when my sister was at work, the spirit spoke to me.

He said, "I knew you could hear me"! He shared a cryptic message for me to deliver to my sister. His message didn't make sense to me. I waited nine months tell her as she didn't believe in that kind of thing. When she heard my words, she thanked me. "You had no way of knowing what his message meant."

Therapy helped me grow stronger, but because I lived in my sister's home, I still wore the mask of her expectations. I was referred to someone for an energy clearing and the person was exceptionally gifted in the ways I needed. The session helped me to see clearly and removed the malevolent energy that I later learned had been attached to me since birth. There I was, helping my sister heal while I lost friends, family, and even the relationship with my children. I knew it was time for me to find my apartment.

Once I moved, my mother's voice grew undeniably loud. I finally listened to what she had to say. She introduced me to my ancestral team. By November, I fully accepted my magic and knew it was time to tell my family of my abilities.

I said, "I'm dying, both figuratively and literally, while you all live your best lives; it stops NOW!" I shared what happened to me as a teenager, something I buried for over thirty years, which resulted in a loop of meeting identical versions of people in different bodies, making the same mistakes, costing me my children.

I faced my challenges head-on, discovering love and compassion for myself. I finally threw away the masks of others' expectations, fully accepting myself unconditionally, flaws and all.

Within three months, I decided it was time to tell the world that I was an intuitive healer and psychic, gifted with most of the clairs. I did so by appearing on a show. The blindfold my mother had placed over my eyes while I was in the void was removed. She wanted me to recognize and operate fully in the beautiful gifts I've been given by the divine.

The love I received after my appearance was profound! I felt what I have always wanted to feel: people loved my light just because of who I AM—not for money, what they could gain from me, my energy, or my resources. I no longer pretended; I was unapologetically myself and who Spirit created and gifted me to be!

Opportunities flooded in. People loved ME, and I only needed to show up as myself. They want to hear my story, and I inspired people with similar challenges. I was no longer ashamed, nor carried guilt. I only needed to believe in the one person I never did –myself! The dreams and desires I'd wished for my entire life are coming to fruition, and with each "yes," there are ten more waiting.

My mother has maintained the promise she made to me in an RTT hypnotherapy session, and she fiercely guides and protects me from the other side of the veil. But she's not alone: four generations of my ancestors, my brother, and my stepfather surrounded me with love and protection that is not bound to time or space. For this, I am overwhelmed with gratitude.

I simply had to be myself, throw away the collection of "masks of expectations," and allow toxic people to fall away. While it wasn't easy, it truly was that simple. I know I am loved unconditionally by people who haven't even met me. I have firm boundaries and standards that I maintain with ease.

THIS is the Tywanah who operates in her gifts, makes no

excuses for her flaws, admits and fixes her mistakes, and guides others from their darkness into the light. Trials come throughout life, but I now choose to say, "What is this teaching me?" rather than "Why is this happening to me?" I send my daughters love and light daily, hoping we'll be reunited someday. I use my voice and help others rediscover theirs.

I lean into the energy and flow with it, not against it. THAT is how my life has changed. I am grateful for this and all that is still yet to come! Like the kintsugi, in my brokenness, the cracks have been filled with gold, making me beautiful, stronger, and more valuable than ever!

Reflection

How have you navigated familial expectations when they've been misaligned with your best interests?

Where have you had cracks in your existence that, once mended, became more beautiful?

When have you claimed sovereignty and given yourself unconditional love? What changed as a result?

CHAPTER THREE

Divinely Guided Relationships

Struck by Serendipity

BARB PRITCHARD

The moment our eyes met, time slowed to a standstill. No one else in the bustling room existed. He stood there, bathed in golden light, and it felt like lightning struck me. Full-body goosebumps enveloped me and took my breath away as if spellbound while a small but mighty, unignorable voice whispered to me, "*This* is your husband."

"Play it cool, Barb. You've got this."

Have you ever seen the musical *Hamilton*? Or heard the song "Satisfied" from it, where Angelica recounted the life-changing moment she met Alexander Hamilton? Looking back, meeting my future husband felt just as impactful. Illuminating. Breathtaking. Time-altering. I didn't realize it then, but it was a Divine line of demarcation. Once crossed, there was no going back.

Justin and I made easy conversation, totally hitting it off. Two introverts who felt at ease with each other, chatting as though no one else was at the party. Somehow, time both stood still and sped forward with such momentum that when we looked up, two hours had passed. I had so much in common with this fantastic, smart, funny, gorgeous, OMG-could-he-really-be-this-freakin'-perfect-for-*me?* man.

What did I do? I told him and my closest friends I couldn't stay; I had a date. No exchange of numbers. No sharing of social media handles. Just a fantastic conversation and an auspiciously aligned connection. *"Not* playing it cool, Barb," my thoughts chided me.

Before that night, I knew that my friends intended to play matchmaker. They told me all about their work colleague Justin: he had a great job, made good money, owned his home, had no kids, and never married. He was also single. All prerequisites for my perfect match, which had been difficult to find in my mid-thirties. In my friends' words, "No flaws detected."

At that time, my friends thought I was still entangled in a long, on-again-off-again, unhealthy relationship with an ex-boyfriend. In reality, I was quite single and had been for months.

They tried before to connect me with other guys, hoping I would see that there were better options out there. While the people they'd tried connecting me with were great, they were just friends. There was never any spark, no romantic synergy kindled.

To thwart their well-intended efforts the night of the party, I'd concocted a story that I had a date scheduled that night. "I'll come for a little while to celebrate your birthday." That way, no one would get their hopes up. No strings, no attachments, and I could go home alone to watch a movie in my PJs on a Saturday night.

In reality, I found it difficult to leave. I *really* liked Justin. We connected on a level that I'd never experienced before. I remember my mother's story about meeting my dad and how she felt like she'd been struck by lightning. *Hello, Barb! This was your once-in-a-lifetime moment where the skies parted, and angels sang!* I was kicking myself as I drove away, but I knew in my heart that this was my path.

I felt if I shared with my friends that I was genuinely single, they would rebuke my ex and praise me for breaking free. I knew that when anyone criticized him, I would instinctively and vehemently defend him—not because he deserved it, but because I was judging myself and feeling ashamed for all the time "wasted" with a guy everyone told me wasn't worthy of me or my time.

In the past, that defense mechanism led me to doubt my heart and make excuses for inexcusable behaviors, believing I wasn't strong enough on my own, which kept me stuck for twelve years in an abusive relationship that was never on my terms. I stuck around because I loved his kid as my own, and the guy had known my dad, my rock before he passed away. My ex was yet another tie to my dad that I was afraid to release—never mind that my dad never liked him. I existed within a cycle of turmoil that dangled the carrot of marriage and approval. Twelve years filled with false hope, manipulation, excuses, abuses of every kind, and feeling like I didn't matter. Months before I met Justin, I'd decided it was time to get off the rollercoaster I'd been riding

My meditation practices and relationship with Spirit empowered me. I felt the need to ensure I was whole. Something much bigger than me told me that time was necessary to move forward with my life. I wasn't hiding; I was healing.

I knew leaving that party was risky. The nagging voice in my head said I blew my chance with a great guy. But my heart told me that pause would be the greatest gift I could give myself and it would be worth it.

In the quiet months of solitude before meeting Justin, I rediscovered myself. I learned to love myself, realizing that I *am* worthy and *more* than enough. I felt creative again, picking up hobbies I'd abandoned years before. I enjoyed my own company and had fun letting my creativity flow. I hung out with my friends, having an active social life not regulated by anyone else. And while I didn't know what would happen with Justin, I knew I wasn't willing to give up the investment in myself for anyone.

So, I left the party, went home, donned my pajamas, and meditated. I grounded myself and asked Spirit to guide my every step.

Nearly three months had passed since I had seen Justin. Without any way to contact him, my only chance to see him was through my friends' gatherings, but Justin's schedule didn't seem to align. Disappointed but at peace with the idea that I may have missed my chance, I continued focusing on healing and my happiness. I meditated daily, spent time with friends, and relished my alone time. When I was ready to start dating, I told my friends that I was single and ready to mingle.

As soon as I felt ready, my friends invited me to their house to decorate for Halloween. To my delight, Justin showed up to help. Just like a cheesy 80s movie, Justin appeared to move in slo-mo, the wind tousling in his hair as he sauntered up the driveway. It was almost excessive how my guides were showing me that was *the* man for me. I've learned they're sassy and have a bold sense of humor.

Justin and I picked right back up where we left off.

Justin is my best friend in every sense of the word. We have the happiest relationship. He believes in me and loves me unconditionally. Without his love, support, and reminders that I'm more than enough and competent, I wouldn't be the confident and secure woman I am today. And I know without a doubt that my dad would approve of Justin.

In hindsight, I owe everything to Spirit. I'm grateful for those not-so-gentle nudges that put me on the path to healing that led me to Justin. Allowing Spirit to lead, I've seen my worth, realized my purpose, ignited my passion, and fueled the flames of transformation for myself and the world through my gifts and skills.

There's always a silver lining—sometimes you may have to squint to see it. Occasionally, circumstances or choices lead us down seemingly perilous paths filled with rocky ravines and shadowy crevices with really *really* sharp edges. But in those darkest times, we should know we're never alone. If we tune in and listen, there's a quiet, still voice that will help us find the strength and courage to move forward. And when you do, it will all be worthwhile.

Our story continues happily: Justin and I will celebrate our sixth wedding anniversary in November 2024.

Reflection

How do you cultivate and listen to your inner voice? What does your intuition feel like physically and emotionally?

What are some key signs that you're ignoring your intuition? How does that show up for you?

Reflect on a decision you made purely based on intuition. What was the outcome?

A Bouquet of White Flowers

EFRAT SHOKEF

It would be our fourth meeting, the first one we intentionally planned to have in this lifetime, at a nearby café. Standing in our driveway, my husband looked into my eyes and said, "You've wanted to meet her forever. If it becomes too much, text me, and I'll be on my way."

Our first meeting in three-dimensional reality had been on January 6, 2011, when our cars crashed, leaving me with one foot out of life and her with one foot in. I was fatally injured, had a near-death experience (NDE), and spent months in the hospital before recovering at home, trying to unravel the invitation my NDE divinely opened. During that time, I strove to find my way back to being the mother of my daughters, slowly learning that it was about the essence of our soul relationship and not about the numerous daily actions I could no longer do.

Our second meeting, a startling, unexpected event, occurred about a year after the car crash. That afternoon, I gathered the courage to drive alone to my physiotherapy session a few minutes away from my parent's house. It felt incredible to be a bit independent.

On my return journey, I took a deep, self-empowering breath

and stopped in a local bookstore for a gift. Walking from the parking lot to the bookstore, I passed a small clothing store and, without a thought, went in. I immediately found a shawl that I knew my sister-in-law wanted. Were those the first signs? Learning to recognize divine signs at the moment they happened, often one leading to another, took me years.

My first solo adventure since the car crash could not have gone more smoothly. It felt good, and I decided that if I was already in a clothing store—maybe I could find something for myself. My physical shape had changed dramatically due to my injuries. Trying anything on was challenging. I still often felt unbalanced, dizzy, and easily tired. It took considerable effort, and I soon regretted the exploration. The seller asked me what had happened, and I shared that I had been in a nearly fatal car crash a year earlier and that day was the first time I had ventured out alone.

I wasn't aware that anyone else was in the store at that time when a woman in the second fitting room said, "I was also involved in a car crash about a year ago." Then, after a few quiet moments, she suddenly asked with a trembling voice, "Can I ask where it happened? What is your name?" Following my confused response, she came out of the fitting room, and whispered, "I think we are from the same story." I was stunned in disbelief.

I asked for her name. It was the only detail I knew, and as she responded, I bent down and sat on the floor, overcome with dizziness. We talked, and before departing, I stood up, and we hugged. As soon as she was out of eyeshot, I erupted into tears. *What just happened?* was my unanswered thought, on repeat.

Bewildered, I lay in bed for three days, crying. It was as if our meeting pushed an emotional release button in my system. Everything I held, the frustration from the healing process, the dramatic changes in our lives, the broken dreams, and my inability to care for my daughters, all gushed out of my eyes and heart.

Years later, the other woman from the same story shared that the questions she asked were just to verify something she already knew. We have never personally met before. How had she known it was me? She just did. Another divinely guided whisper?

Our third meeting took place a few weeks later in court. This time, we knew the other, would also be there. We were not to talk with one another. I quietly stole glances at her, still curious and wondering. A seed of soul recognition within me, germinated.

Time passed, and I thought about her a lot. I wanted to send her a bouquet of white flowers, which I never did. Although she was found responsible for the crash, I knew she wasn't to blame, and I desperately needed her to know that I knew that. Why? The reasons had yet to merge into my awareness.

Over the next three years, I significantly recovered. I returned to my academic work, only to realize I could no longer do it nor wanted to. I found my way back to mothering my daughters, although it was different from before.

The vision of a bouquet of white flowers continued to visit my thoughts with various imagined scenarios. I had to meet her—intentionally meet her. The universe expressed its intention, and now it was up to us to take it forward and enter the door of opportunity. I did not know why or what I expected. I just had a strong inner knowing that I had to reach out. I prepared mentally and changed my mind countless times until the date was set for our fourth meeting: January 5, 2015—our first intentional one.

On my drive to the café, my heart beat fiercely. I had envisioned bringing a bouquet of white flowers with me so many times, but I did not. I arrived early and sat waiting. The café was fairly empty, and I was happy about that.

As I saw her hesitantly walking closer, I couldn't help but ask myself, *What are you thinking?* But then, as I looked into her soft eyes, I felt something I had never felt before—a profound recognition and knowing, tranquil and divine. I knew her. I know her, and she knows me. Not the knowing of our physical beings of the present with names and looks, but the knowing of souls. From before, from the after, beyond space and time.

The feeling blew my mind. If this was how I felt, could it be that the crash was actually an act of profound soul love? A divine intervention and synchronicity on its own? Was our soul connection the "unknown cause" in creating our meaningful encounters?

We embraced in a long hug, and all my fears from our meeting vanished immediately. We talked and got to know the here and now of us. We learned what each of us went through over those four years since our crash into one another in this lifetime.

It was the first meeting of many. As I embraced the gifts offered to me in my NDE, she joined my classes and group sessions. She is a magnificent healer. Every time we meet, my heart opens wider with gratitude and love. Sometimes, we share with others who we are for one another. Sometimes, we just keep it between us: a seed of profound soul connection, nourishing us by our shared co-existence in the here and now. In retrospect, both of us, know in our hearts, that all of our unforeseen meetings were divinely orchestrated, inviting our souls, to connect, and nudge each other to become.

Recently, one spring morning, when the star jasmine surrounding our house, dressed up in its white bloom and its sweet and wild scent, filled the air, I realized I needed to ask, *"Who was this bouquet of white flowers symbolically for? Was it an image communicated to me through the field, like songs we suddenly sing to ourselves, or a thought about another, inviting our human action? Was it for her? Or was it for me? Who did I ask to see, embrace, and forgive?"* I looked closely at the flowers, their star, wheel-like shape. I inhaled the perfumed air, and my eyes filled with tears.

The bouquet was also about forgiving myself and developing trust that everything is held and guided. It was yet another gift from Heaven, reminding me that I am never alone, also here, in the most unexpected encounters, ones we might perceive as negative in earthly ways.

Every so often, those who challenge us the most are part of a written invitation and are actually the ones who greatly love us. I, too, prefer the positive signs posted along our journey—the numbers, the songs, and the enjoyable invitations. However, time and again, three-dimensional human events we may perceive as negative, like my car crash, are just as powerful synchronicities—an invitation to explore, to dare, and to become.

Reflection

Who does your heart wish to offer a bouquet of white flowers to?

What challenging phases or steps in your journey can you forgive yourself for taking?

Is there someone you wish to be grateful to for offering you an opportunity for growth, even if, at the human level, it may all seem like a negative sequence of synchronicities?

The Birthday Card

YVETTE LEFLORE

"Send him a birthday card," said the voice in my head.

I knew the voice meant my ex-husband because it was early October, just a week before our wedding anniversary and a few weeks before his birthday. We'd been divorced for seven years and hadn't spoken since. My face squished with confusion, and I ignored the voice.

Days later, the voice repeated. *"Send him a birthday card!"* I asked, "Why would I do this?" He was my ex-husband. I'd asked for a divorce because he was a person with an alcohol use disorder who had turned to other drugs and left me in debt. Although I'd done a lot of work on myself, I was still harboring anger and grief. *Why* would I send him a birthday card? It made no sense, but the voice urged on, and although I wasn't fully aware, like I am today, that this voice was Divine's whisper, I finally listened.

I scoured the aisles in the store, looking for a birthday card to send to this man, whom I hadn't spoken to in years. I had no idea what was happening in his life. Was he remarried? Did he have children? Where was he living? There were no cards for this situation. I settled upon a blank card with a picture of an orange tabby resembling the cat we'd had together. I don't remember what I wrote, but I signed it from the cat, Taffy, and me and sent it to his parents' address. I packed my suitcase and headed off for a week in Mexico for relaxation and a seminar on men, women, and relationships.

A week later, at the end of October, I walked through the kitchen door, tanned, relaxed, and revitalized after a week of fun, sun, and energizing conversation. I dropped my suitcase and, with my coat still on, shuffled through the mail sitting on the kitchen table. There it was: a card with his writing and return address in the corner. I felt my heart beating in my throat. A part of me never expected a note back. I'd answered the bidding of the voice and thought I'd completed the task. Curiosity got the better of me. I took a deep breath and ripped it open.

Thank you so much for writing. It means the world to me. I just got out of the hospital. I have lung cancer, and they removed part of my lung and some ribs. I'm staying with my parents. Pete

The letter dropped out of my hands onto the table. I felt emotion well up, but I pushed it back down. Numbness crept through me as I tried to process what I'd read. I wasn't clear about what I was feeling. My mind was a whirlwind of thoughts, but the central theme was: "What do I do now?" I was paralyzed with emotions, present to both fear and a thread of love that had never dissipated. And so, I did what was most comfortable; I ignored it the best I could.

As I pretended the note had never arrived, the words I'd read would waft in like an unwanted scent, and I'd open the door to let fresh air in so I could forget. For a month, I struggled with what to do and how to proceed. I wasn't sure there was *anything* I wanted to do with this information, but how could I ignore it? He was a man I had loved and who had loved me. After our divorce, and with the help of a therapist, a 12-step program for relatives of addicts, and other programs, I realized I'd never really let him love me. I'd shut out his love and blamed our divorce on his addiction, yet I'd never taken the time to tell him this. So, finally, after Thanksgiving, I dialed his parents' number. I stood there with the phone cord wrapping in and out of my fingers, listening to the phone ring and waiting for someone to pick it up.

His mother answered and was as delightful as I remembered, although sadness seeped through her words. She shared that he was in the hospital, but yes, I could visit him. She was sure he'd want to see me.

I walked down the hospital hallway a day later, looking for his room. My breath was shallow, and I swallowed involuntarily, as I do when I'm nervous. I saw his room number and a man in the bed who looked about seventy years old. I stepped back and rechecked the number on the door to ensure I was in the correct place. My mind could not comprehend the dissonance between the man I saw in the bed, who looked seventy, and the forty-seven-year-old he was.

As I quietly walked toward the bed, he turned his head and said, "Hey, hon." Tears welled in my eyes as I walked over, sat in the chair, and took his hand. I kept my emotions in check as we caught up. As I left, he asked if I'd return, and I assured him I would. I barely made it to my car before the emotions flooded out of me. I sat in the car and sobbed. I grieved for what we never got to have because we each had our wounds. I grieved for the pain he was currently enduring.

During December, I visited Pete a couple of times a week. We spoke of memories, laughed, and mostly sat in silence. During many visits, he was sleeping, so I held his hand or touched his arm to let him know I was there. Our wounds were healing during that time. Whether they healed during conversation or just in our presence with one another, they healed. Hurtful things had been said and done in the past on both parts, but we didn't need to speak of them. All we needed to do was be in one another's energy for healing to occur. It felt like a tapestry was being repaired, and the holes where the wounds once tore the fabric were stitched together with every visit.

His family welcomed my hospital visits and urged me to stay and spend time with them as well. During this time, I discovered he'd never married again and that I'd been his one true love. They told me how much he'd loved me even after we divorced. There was a duality of sadness and comfort in receiving that information. Even though we were healing the past, I knew I didn't want a future with him. This sacred time together was about healing.

At the end of December, I walked into his hospital room, and they were preparing to send him home. I waited for him at his parents' house. Once he arrived, he was exhausted, and we visited long enough for me to tell him I'd come to see him again when I returned from a business trip. When I look back, I know I didn't understand how close to death he was. Upon my return, I called to see how and where he was, and his brother told me he had died. I hung up the phone and sobbed. I didn't get to say that final goodbye.

Although I never got that final physical connection or an opportunity to attend his funeral, I always considered myself blessed for our opportunity to heal. Looking back, I'm grateful that Divine didn't give up on me. Instead, the voice persisted, and once I listened, Divine revealed the next step. It was like following the path of crumbs in the woods to find my way out of the darkness to heal at a deeper level.

I'd done much personal work, but Divine knew the beauty was in the relationship work. Pete and I were able to mend the hurts during his time on earth so I could accept him as part of my angel team. He's been an active part of my angel team since his death, and maybe he's too active sometimes. At one point, I had to set boundaries to keep him from interfering with my dating life. He has lent his loving support from the other side and was even joyous about my second marriage. Periodically, I hear his laugh and know he's with me. I'm forever grateful to the voice that whispered, *"Send him a birthday card."*

Reflection

Write about a time you received a sudden knowing that you had to do something. Did you follow-through? What was the outcome?

Write a love letter to a past significant other. What would you want them to know now?

Reflect on a time that you reconnected with someone who had been important in your life. What was that experience like? What did you learn about yourself through it?

Divine Miracles: God's Perfect Timing

DONNA BURGHER

The house was dark, except for a faint glow seeping through a barely closed door. That was where you could find me, slumped on the couch night after night, legs propped up on the coffee table, mindlessly watching reruns on Nick-at-Nite. At least I wasn't alone. I had my two best friends. Ben… and…Jerry. *Was this really my life?*

My daily wardrobe had become sweats and T-shirts, so imagine my excitement when I put on makeup and went out for dinner with my husband, Bob, who was visiting town for the weekend. Right before dessert came, I looked into my husband's eyes as I quietly shared how lonely and unhappy I was; tears welled and rolled down my cheeks.

We decided to move from Michigan to California for a promotion leading to professional and financial rewards. I fully supported my husband as he successfully climbed the corporate ladder. After a year of living in California, our daughter, Michelle, was miserable, and so was I. My husband and I weighed the pros and cons. We decided that Michelle and I would move back to Michigan into our home so she could finish high school with her friends. The plan included Bob joining us in Michigan after the lease on the townhouse we rented was up. That never happened.

Bob and I were high school sweethearts and best friends. We dated for five years before we got married. My twenty-year-old self was excited for our future. We both wanted a family. Two years after we wed, our son was born. Our second child arrived three years later; five years after that, we had Michelle.

My first divine calling was to be a mom. The plan was for us to raise our children and grow old together.

Living apart from my husband made me feel like a single parent. Unfortunately, due to toxic mold exposure, Michelle was unhealthy, which meant I was on call 24/7. Doctor appointments, tests, and emergency hospital stays were my norm. Doing it alone took a toll on me.

I had no plans, no dreams, no vision. One day merged into the next.

It was just another gray winter day, so I grabbed a blanket and entered the family room. I was resting on the couch when I received a "call" and heard, "Donna, we don't recognize you. You are an empty shell of a woman."

In hindsight, that was a divine wake-up call. I remember getting up and walking into the hallway, where the sun was streaming through the glass doors. I yearned for more. More happiness, fun, love, and joy. What I once envisioned as my forever life no longer resembled my current reality. With tears streaming down my face, I looked up, declaring to God, "I want to start over." I had no clue what that would look like at that time, but God had a plan.

Over the next couple of weeks, my energy and motivation shifted. It felt like a switch had been flipped, and I began to experience the most amazing levels of love, joy, and bliss. I easily shed the extra weight; it's just melted away. Bye-bye, Ben and Jerry

A few months after I declared that I wanted to start over, I woke up to the sound of rain. But when I looked out my window, the sky was blue. I headed downstairs, following the sound. I stopped on the landing, where I saw a stream of water flowing down my driveway. As my foot hit the cold marble floor, I stepped into a mini lake. In the laundry room, I was shocked to see a geyser had erupted from the washing machine hose. I found the shut-off valve, turned it, and the water stopped flowing.

Why does it still sound like it's raining?

Like a detective, I followed the sound again. I cautiously walked down to our fully furnished lower level. With each step, the carpet got wetter and wetter. When I reached the bottom, I stood there in disbelief. Water was pouring down from the ceiling.

I immediately hired a company, but they failed to dry out the house, leaving us with toxic mold. Michelle and I moved into a hotel during remediation but never returned to our home.

Another company was hired. As I explained what had happened to the owner, his head technician arrived. With a clipboard in hand, he began walking up my drive. His head was down until he got to the garage. He lifted his head, and our eyes met. In my spirit, I instantly sensed something. We were introduced, and as time passed, we became friends. Bob knew about him. The three of us went out a couple of times just to hang out. But then there was a shift. I asked for a divorce, and I moved forward in this new relationship. We started a company and life together during my separation. That did not go well with my children.

After Michelle graduated from high school, she decided to move back to California to live with her dad instead of with me. About a year later, Bob called to tell me that Michelle was visiting her friends in Michigan. He said, "She is not ready to see you."

Heartbroken, I fell into bed, sobbing. Half a box of tissues later, I decided that somehow, some way, I would see her. I prayed and believed it would happen, but I had no clue when or how.

The entire week went by, and nothing happened. It was Michelle's last day in town, and our day was filled with appointments.

Before we even left the house, someone called to reschedule. As we drove to our first appointment, they rescheduled, and then the last one canceled. After our busy day was unexpectedly cleared, we looked at each other, wondering what we wanted to do with our free time.

We decided to go to one of our favorite stores, even though it was forty-five minutes away. We walked in, and I immediately headed toward the glass-covered counter. Leaning in to view its contents, I felt tap, tap. I turned around, and there she was, my daughter, standing in front of me, crying. I opened my arms, and we hugged.

We stepped outside into the hot, humid air to talk.

Michelle said, "I wasn't even planning on coming here today, and then, at the last minute, I decided to come with my friends. We arrived just minutes before you."

I said, "I wasn't planning on coming here today either. Our schedule changed at the last minute."

Over several years, our family experienced devastating times, which led to our once close-knit, loving family becoming estranged. Michelle asked, "Why did all this have to happen?"

I looked into her tear-filled eyes and said, "I don't know. But I believe one day God will reveal it to us." We held each other tight, said how much we loved one another and returned to the air-conditioned store. I hugged her friends, and we visited for a bit. Then we parted ways. Michelle had a plane to catch.

Unbeknownst to us, God had a plan.

At the last minute, we had both been divinely guided to the same store, arriving just minutes apart. Driving home that day, my heart was filled with love and gratitude. God is amazing. Our encounter was miraculous, a serendipitous moment that only God could have orchestrated.

God knew what He was doing in reconnecting Michelle and me

because the period afterward was far from rainbows and lollipops. In fact, the most difficult years I've yet experienced unfolded in ways I would never have imagined. With each turn came a different twist. The guy who walked up my drive and I parted ways.

I thank God daily for renewing my relationship with my daughter, which is filled with unconditional love.

Through God's love and grace, He healed my heart and renewed my mind. As I walk in faith, I trust in God's plans for my life and in His perfect timing.

Reflection

Reflect on a time when you felt lost or disconnected from your true self. What events or realizations helped you begin to find your way back to a place of happiness and purpose?

Have you ever experienced a moment of synchronicity or divine intervention that felt too perfectly timed to be a coincidence? Describe the experience and how it impacted your life.

Think about a challenging period in your life. How did you see God guiding you through it? In what ways did this experience transform you or bring unexpected blessings?

Angel in Disguise
DAWN MICHELE JACKSON

My heart was broken. The shocking words, "I want a divorce," sounded foreign to me. *He must be joking. Things have been rough for a while, but we made a vow to one another. We have a three-year-old son and I'm only thirty. This isn't how the story is supposed to end. My husband is one of the kindest men I know; surely, he's going to change his mind.*

I remember back when we met in 1992. It was an extremely painful time but a year that changed the trajectory of my life. At the time I didn't see how crossing paths with one individual would save me in more ways than one. Looking back, I now know that sometimes angels show up in our lives just when we need them the most.

For years, I'd been in a toxic relationship that had consumed my life through high school and my first three years of college. I felt stuck, afraid, and unsure how to remove myself from the situation. The emotional and verbal abuse wore me down, but the physical abuse scared me the most. Every time I tried to leave it got worse. When I finally had enough, he showed up at my parents' house. I was terrified as he pounded on the sliding glass door yelling at me. Had my stepdad not appeared at just the right moment, I'm not sure what would have happened. That was truly the last straw for me.

In previous months, my longtime hairdresser had been telling me about her brother who would soon be getting out of the military. She wanted us to meet. I was skeptical, as I was already in a relationship that I was desperately trying to get out of, but I agreed to meet up with her and her brother for Oktoberfest.

Feeling nervous about meeting someone new, I anxiously wondered what would happen if my current boyfriend found out. Honestly, it was hard to trust anyone new based on what I'd been going through but it didn't take long to see how this man was different. His energy was kind, polite, caring, and compassionate from the moment I laid eyes on him. There was a quiet side but there was also a goofy side that loved to laugh and have fun. I somehow felt that his presence was there to help me let go of something that was destroying me. And I intuitively knew that in letting go of my previous relationship I would be okay, and my life would improve. I just couldn't see what the future would hold.

Our relationship blossomed, we moved in together, got married, and had a child. We had our struggles as neither one of us was truly ready for what a long-term relationship entailed. He went directly from high school to the military before meeting me. I went from an unhealthy relationship to trying to navigate a relationship with him. We tried our hardest, but my heart was filled with a great deal of pain for which I didn't have the tools to heal. My heart had been injured in my previous relationship and I expected my husband to pick up the pieces. No matter how hard he tried he couldn't heal or fix what had happened earlier in my life; that was my work to do.

Once my husband made the decision that he wanted a divorce, no amount of counseling, crying, or begging changed his mind. The days that immediately followed were a blur. I did what had to be done but couldn't muster the strength to do much more. Nights were filled with tearful phone calls to my best friend and my mom going over the same thing time and time again, all the while hoping that he'd change his mind. He didn't.

I didn't know how to move forward. My identity was tied to being a wife, mom, and nurse. *Who was I beyond these roles?* I had no idea nor any desire to find out. I just wanted my life back and for some time I thought I could somehow make it happen. I believed that because we had a child together things would work out for us, but I had no idea how that would even come about. All I knew was that my life took a dramatic detour from the "white picket fence" life I'd dreamed about since I was a little girl. I was devastated. In my anger, I blamed my husband for the demise of our marriage. In my mind, he was another person abandoning me which felt unbearable. *What was wrong with me?*

As the divorce process moved forward, I continued to blame my husband, saying that he had given up, was unwilling to work on our marriage, and that he didn't care about breaking up our family. I believed all this to be true while neglecting to see my role in the dissolution of our marriage. I failed to see how much he was hurting or to take credit for my part. All I could see was that he walked away. He even left me with the house and most things inside of it except his personal belongings, but that didn't matter much to me either.

For months, I chose to be miserable, stuck in my grief. After finally seeing a therapist, I realized I had two choices: continue to be miserable or start to heal all that was hurting my heart. Thankfully, I chose the latter. It started with venturing out and doing stuff beyond my comfort zone including international medical mission trips, meeting new people, and truly enjoying life again. I had forgotten what it felt like to feel joy and for a bit of time, this helped me move forward and forget about my pain.

After a while though, I noticed that despite these distractions, my heart still hurt. *How could I feel better? What did I need to do to heal?* I started searching for answers as I knew that there was more to life than the pain I'd been stuck in for years. One open door led to another as I immersed myself in retreats and workshops, reading spiritual books, and connecting with those who helped me clear out the cobwebs and find the light again. Once I started, I never stopped as I kept searching and discovering new parts of me, parts that had been hidden by pain. I learned to heal the grief that had filled my heart and kept me from living the life I dreamed about. I felt whole for the first time in my life.

The deeper the healing the more I realized that my husband was the one who had saved my life in many ways throughout my life. Not only had he swept in to help me leave a truly toxic relationship and guide me to safety, but he left me when it was time for me to find myself. His exit was the catalyst for my healing and becoming the woman I am today. This discovery has been full of many tears, apologies, and gratitude for the angel who dropped into my life to lead me to safety and then let me go so I could find my wings and fly again. A divine angel in disguise!

I believe that we don't drop into each other's lives haphazardly. There is always a purpose but sometimes it takes time to discover that purpose. We often serve as messengers for one another and show up to guide others to their highest selves. Today my gratitude goes above and beyond any pain that occurred during my marriage and divorce; all of it has been a gift. People are often amazed at how my ex-husband and I co-parent with such ease, kindness, and support for one another. I smile with the knowing that a divine plan had been in place all along, I just couldn't see it at the time!

Reflection

Reflecting on struggles in your own life what are/were they here to teach you?

Who in your life has been an angel in disguise and how did they assist you?

Looking back, what experiences that were initially a struggle in your life, can you now view as a gift?

I Got You

CAROLYN MARIE

As I sit here to share my story, it seems like a completely different person was living my life so long ago. But she was no stranger; it was me, the single mom now empty nester feeling lost and missing the hustle and bustle of the kids' events, spring soccer games, ice cold mornings spent in equally cold skating rinks. Then there was the make-up and the dreaded eyelashes, the application of which never ended well, along with numerous costume changes for my daughter's dance recitals. Oh, how I missed it all.

What now? Where to? Who am I now? I had no idea I was a lost soul feeling broken, battered, defeated, and so very alone. I desperately needed a change. I can feel the emptiness and darkness as I revisit that time in my mind. I almost can't find the words to describe what was inside of me, a numbness, and I yearned for a way out. I could have starred in *Eat, Pray, Love*, my favorite movie ever. I felt her pain. I needed to see the light again, and I needed to feel it again. I, too, felt dead inside.

Meanwhile, life's hits kept coming fast and furiously, providing no solace for my weary soul. My life resembled the whack-a-mole, that carnival game where every time a poor, unexpecting mole came up for air and light, BAM! it got smacked on the head and knocked back down again. Yup, that was me. It wasn't one life-threatening tragedy; it was a series of seemingly never-ending life challenges and struggles overtaking my breath and my life. Depression and anxiety, I found out, are very real. I was tired of rowing the boat against the current alone. Finances, house repairs, unexpected bills, and children struggling to find their way were things I just couldn't separate from. It simply wasn't a skill I had at the time. I found myself exhausted scrambling to figure it all out and was losing hope.

I remember it as if it was yesterday, sitting at my café-style kitchen table and looking out my deck door. It was a cold, gray Sunday morning during the early shutdowns of COVID-19. I felt so alone and broken. I wanted someone—anyone to—tell me things would be okay. As I sat there with a river of tears streaming down my face, wishing I had someone who had my back. I cried out, "I'm so done I don't want to do this anymore!" I wanted so badly to know I wasn't alone. Someone to put their arm around me and tell me "I got you." In my heart I felt it. I knew it wasn't a friend or any one person giving me well-intended advice. This energy felt bigger a powerful loving presence. In that moment, I had this buzzing jolt I needed to get to church, and I needed to go right then. I felt these feelings so deeply in my being that I couldn't ignore it. I knew I needed to get to a church, and it wasn't the church I belonged to and hadn't been to in twenty years. It was someplace different. I frantically started to Google "churches near me." Services were about to begin, and I wanted to be certain I made it! I did! I arrived at the church that had beckoned me to it as if my car drove itself. *There are no coincidences. Buckle up, buttercup, get inside.* Man plans; God laughs.

The congregation wasn't large, and it felt like *Cheers* where everyone knew each other's names. I tried to hide in the background. But a new face was spotted: mine! A lovely, elderly woman sat on one side of me and a bearded young man on the other. The soft spirit-filled music began to play as attendees rose for the service to begin. A well of emotion poured over me. I felt a gentle touch on my right hand from the woman sitting beside me as she placed her hand on mine, providing comfort. I felt an overwhelming sense of love. My eyes closed, tears still streaming, when someone touched me on my shoulder, and said in a gentle, masculine voice, "I got you." I could not believe I had just heard those words—the very words I longed so badly to hear. I knew it was God using this young man to deliver His message directly to me. God had (and has) my back! More tears. At that moment, I knew I wasn't alone, and I never had been. I could breathe and hope filled me. I never saw that young man again nor visited that church, but these words became a signpost for me ever since that day: "I got you."

I began to trust again. I made choices to change my life. First, I chose to surrender everything. This was my call to action, and the signposts showed up to guide me along my journey. I sold my home, I let go of all my material possessions and most courageously I released the identities I held onto for too long. My new plan was to trust and have faith there was a plan. Patience was key. It was a long process but one that was being divinely guided.

No longer am I the woman of my past desperate at the kitchen table. I am rebirthing, reinventing and rediscovering what sets my soul on fire to make this next chapter of life the very best chapter!

I began to say YES to me, and NO to fear. I moved into trust and surrendered the "how's". I trusted God had a plan for me and my only job was to say "yes" when an opportunity was presented. The net comes after the leap every time. Each yes, another door opened and crazy as it may sound those three small but mighty words "I got you" showed up to validate the way every time in books, out of stranger's mouths, on t-shirts all at the perfect moment as an answer to my inquiries. These words have ignited my courage, deepened my faith and have led me to step up into brighter days, bigger and better than I could have ever imagined. I chose to trust the breadcrumbs guiding me to a life I love, living my purpose sharing my story to be a light for someone along the way to know they too are never alone. Your sign may and most likely will be different from mine, yet it will be divinely perfect for you.

A few years have passed since those darks days as I write this story 37,000 feet in the air on the way to my next adventure to learn, to grow, to laugh and connect with other amazing women to be more of who we are meant to be. I am living courageously, authentically, discovering more of who I am and what I have to contribute in the world feeling aligned, supported, and guided back to JOY.

I share my story to encourage the knowing not all who wander are lost and that you are never alone. We are all being divinely guided. I couldn't have imagined how my life would unfold from those dark days. I guess it wasn't for me to imagine but to continue following the inner nudges that know exactly how to show me the way of my heart and soul. Be open to noticing the signs. Your entire life just may become an amazing, wild ride of magical moments, signs, and synchronicities. My soul was waiting for the YES. Your soul is waiting for the YES.

It is my hope you always remember these words "I Got You." Release fear and say yes, do the thing that is calling you and feel the wings on your heart take flight. You are never alone. I Got YOU!

Reflection

Take a moment to describe a recent experience where you noticed a sign or synchronicity? How did it make you feel?

How do you think paying attention to divine signs and synchronicities can impact your decision making?

Journal about a time when you felt a strong sense of alignment or flow in your life. Were there any signs or synchronicities that stood out during that time? What meaning do they hold for you?

Finding Self Love

LAURIE BURKHALTER

For so many years, I searched for self-love and couldn't figure out why I didn't feel it or know how to get it.

Just out of high school, I met and married a man who was physically and emotionally abusive. He didn't want to spend much time with me and our three beautiful daughters. I found out later that he had a drug problem. Although he went to rehab, his abusive behavior didn't stop. We had been together for eight years when I finally filed for divorce.

I relocated to Las Vegas and decided that I just wanted to have fun without being in a serious relationship. There, I finally realized that we had become close friends and entered a serious love relationship. She gave me so much attention, which is what I so much desired, but she ended up being very controlling, jealous, and physically abusive. I finally ended it and moved back to California.

I attracted so many verbally, emotionally, and physically abusive relationships, both friends and lovers, which reinforced my lack of self-love. Friends often said, "Do you feel like you can love yourself?" I tried, even going as far as to take an empowerment course. Saying to my mirrored reflection, "I love you," felt disingenuous, resulting in me dissolving into tears.

After years of going in and out of abusive and narcissistic relationships, I met and married a woman in 2015. Together, we had a daughter before that relationship devolved into one that brought me to my knees. My former wife, as our daughter's biological mother, discouraged my involvement despite my being listed as the other parent on the birth certificate. During this painful time, I sought therapy.

It was in therapy that I realized that I was the common denominator in all my bad relationships. "Why am I attracted to people who want to hurt me?" I asked. "These relationships are destructive to me and my friends and family." These realizations started a shift, which continued as I gave up my thirty-year massage therapy practice.

"Have you considered life coaching or some other kind of coaching?" my therapist asked.

Life coaching. That notation really resonated with me. I focused first on becoming a certified crystal healer before I was introduced to an elemental archetypal astrology coaching practice.

I've always loved astrology, helping others heal and transform their lives. With this practice, I could support others in healing from the inside out. The blessing in all of this was that while I supported others, I learned, too, and underwent my own transformation.

As part of this program, along with Lisa Michaels's work, I learned about my creation team and how each team player connects to help me align with my life's purpose. The next level went deeper, and I had a session directly with Lisa. She had me visualize all the way back to my mother's womb. Then we went a step further, and Lisa asked me to return to where I was before I decided I wanted to be in this life. I asked my spirit guides to be with me, and they helped me see that I had come here to be a healer. At that moment, all I had been through started to make sense.

Lisa had me return to the womb to see and feel what my biological mother experienced. I felt her deep love for me and that she had been in turmoil over having to choose me, her unborn baby, or her older children. That was the early 1960s, and my birth mother, who had been separated from her husband, had an affair. I was the result of that affair. If she had chosen to keep me, she might have lost her parental rights to her older children. My birth mother kept her pregnancy and my birth a secret. I felt her pain and shame and realized it wasn't only me; it was also about the affair.

Lisa had me send Love to my unborn self, bathing me in pink light and pure Love. Then, she had me send love to my biological mom. Love radiated for both of us. I could see and feel my mother's love for me; I finally forgave her. I felt that she had already died, but her spirit held on because of her shame. With my forgiveness, she was free to move on.

Then, I witnessed myself being born. My birth mom gave birth to me by herself, cleaned both of us and drove to the hospital where she was giving me up for adoption. I saw her sobbing as she handed me to the nurses, all of them cooing and making a fuss over me. I felt so much Love and attention. From there, my mom and dad adopted me, and they were so happy to have me.

When Lisa brought me back to the present, for the first time in my life, I felt true love, the color of pink, filling every cell of my body. My shame had dissipated. I burst into joyful tears.

I had been carrying that shame my whole life. With Lisa's support, I saw my mother, my biological mother, and the love she had for me. I realized that I wasn't rejected but was truly loved.

Being able to love myself truly has given me such an inner peace. Now, when hardships happen, I can see through the lens of love and deal with life's ups and downs much better. I have attracted better relationships, lost over fifty pounds of emotional weight, and attracted better clients. All this, plus I continue to manifest more money in my life.

I expanded once I discovered the self-love I had long been searching for. And wow, it's such a fantastic gift to have! Now, I coach people how to give themselves the self-love they deserve, love others deeply, and connect with themselves honestly.

Reflection

How do you show yourself self-love and how does it feel? In what areas of your life could you improve your self-love?

In what circumstances do you prioritize your needs and desires over that of your partner or family?

When has a lack of self-love impacted your life negatively? What did you learn about that experience upon reflection?

CHAPTER FOUR

Following Signs & Synchronicities

Consciously Orchestrating a Life-Changing Move

KAREN SHIER

I'm fortunate to have owned several homes; however, purchasing or selling each was always stressful, caused anxiety-inducing what-if thinking, attracted few showings, took many months, and usually resulted in a financial loss. I was stuck in my money stories, and it seemed I always sold in a down market, often losing money on the home improvements I made, resulting in more of the same lack feelings and expectations.

I grudgingly felt that whether I was the buyer or seller, the realtor never worked in my best interest. I'd allow myself to get mired in the what-ifs of the deal. What if the deal fell through? What if the interest rate was too high? What if there were hidden dangers that the home inspector couldn't see? What if I lost my job and couldn't afford the payment? What if a tree fell on the place after I moved in? These were the inner critic whisperings I'd wrestle with in my first few decades as a homeowner.

Then something extraordinary happened. I found an amazing life partner, and we planned to marry and sell our homes in different cities. In 2015, we found and purchased our joint home.

My husband and I believed we were purchasing our forever home, a tired fifty-something-year-old ranch-style home that needed some tender loving care and thousands of dollars to bring it up to code and to what we envisioned it to be for us as our first home together as a married couple. It was on top of a hill on a beautiful private lake surrounded by trees and nature, peaceful and quiet.

We discovered that quiet summer mornings brought us a lake surface like glass and the occasional call of a pair of loons. We also had the best sunset views on the lake, which overlooked a dam and was unobstructed by other homes around us. In autumn, our home was suspended like a tree house and immersed in the beauty of fall colors casting brilliant reflections on the lake. In the winter, the snow blanketed our abode in loveliness and solitude. We didn't realize it then, but we had unconsciously created and manifested this lovely home.

We were both experienced in purchasing fixer-uppers and could see past all of the work that needed to be done. After a moment of pinching ourselves at finally getting through the negotiating and months of anxiously waiting for the sellers to let it go to closing and the stresses of fixing and selling our two other pre-marital homes, we got right to work on moving in.

When we acquired this lovely place on a lake, my husband was often traveling internationally and not home very much. I was working at a company about fifteen minutes away. It made sense to purchase this home closer to my work since I'd commute daily, and he was often away.

We enjoyed this home for eight years when life happened again. On a Saturday ride to the Lake Michigan lakeshore, we made a "just-like-that" decision to adapt again. We decided to move my husband closer to work to cut down his hours' long daily commute, alleviate his constant exhaustion, and get a little more of his life back. I could work from anywhere since I had retired from my corporate job and was now working from home.

This move was going to be different, though. It would not be filled with worry, doubt, mistrust, and what-ifs that had been part of my experience. We consciously created what our lives would look like. We agreed to be very clear on our intentions about where we wanted to be and to trust and surrender to what may come our way, not limiting our possibilities by insisting it look or happen a certain way.

I started with the inner work to overcome my fears from the past. I journaled daily to the Universe, to God, the Angels, and Spirit Guides—what I call my Divine Support Team. I let my team know how I wanted the sale of our home and purchase of our new home to flow with ease and grace. I surrendered to them to allow our move to happen at just the right timing.

My husband and I took inspired actions as we engaged in the co-creation of our new direction. Simply put, we worked to prepare our home for the market.

For twelve straight days, we power-washed and painted the house and decks. We completed outdoor projects we had been meaning to do. We selected and met with our new realtor and shared our intentions with him. We rejected his preconceived notion that our house would be hard to sell to a family because of the layout. And we had purchased it, hadn't we? We held space that other couples would also be interested.

We engaged a professional stager who gave us a list of what seemed like 101 things to do to ready our home for listing. We adopted her excellent suggestions to showcase our home in the best light to would-be buyers. We packed, painted, sorted, and toothbrush-cleaned the entire house. We were ready.

The whole process happened so quickly. Pictures were taken on Monday. We listed the home on Tuesday and had three showings the first day it was on the market. On Wednesday, we had six showings. Thursday, more people came through.

We received three full-price-plus offers on Thursday evening, a dream come true and a unique, joyful experience for both of us. The

Universe returned to us a lovely and aligned buyer couple who promised no drama and everything to flow easily and gracefully.

On Friday afternoon, we drove excitedly to our new city and joyfully placed a deposit on a new home in a mixed dwelling community we'd selected that was only ten minutes from my husband's workplace. The market was hot for the houses in this development, but again our luck held enabling us to grab one of the last two houses in that sought-after community.

We happily learned the construction schedule on our new home was perfectly aligned with our lake house sale so we wouldn't have to wrangle multiple moves and storage units. Thank you, Universe!

It just so happened that our new home was sided in one of two colors we love, and the interior colors that were already planned matched our current furniture and décor perfectly. It was a lovely surprise since we could not pick out those spec home items personally. Thank you again, Universe!

On Saturday, the inspections on our lake home passed with flying colors, and we learned that our buyers intended to proceed with the purchase. A month later, both of our closings happened in the same week.

Looking back, it all seems so surreal. From what we thought was our dream lake home to a weekend moving decision and a brand-new home adventure on the horizon in just six weeks. We adapted, set our intentions, surrendered, and trusted that all would flow smoothly with ease and grace. And it did!

We went into this with crystal clear intentions and treated it like a Law of Attraction experiment. We put what I've learned to work. We visualized. I journaled daily, talked to my Divine Support Team, and asked that our move happen in just the right timing. We focused on what we wanted instead of what we didn't.

When I heard a whisper from my inner critic of what might go wrong, I immediately soothed her, consciously shifting my thoughts. Lower-level thoughts weren't welcomed into my energy field. I didn't allow myself to engage with the worry mind as I would have done in the past.

We didn't limit the outcomes. We intended, trusted, and surrendered. We consciously co-created what we wanted to happen. Our Divine Support Team brought us something even better than we imagined.

Today, we are grateful to be in our new home. My husband has gotten more of his life back, and I am grateful to have witnessed his joy. We are enjoying this new adventure closer to Lake Michigan. I'm unsure if this is our new forever home, but we are excited and open to the next Divine chapter of synchronicity.

Reflection

Can you recall a time in your life when you consciously decided to approach things differently than you would have in the past? How did that work out for you?

Can you recall a time that you allowed yourself to trust and surrender to feelings of a situation working out just right instead of pushing against or trying to control the situation? How did it feel?

Have you ever talked with your inner critic when she is bringing up fears and untruths to your awareness?

Braving Wings

BY AMBER KASIC

Driving the winding roads displaying the fullness of autumn's colors, I smiled knowing my dad was with me, somewhere between the oscillating rays of sun and the shadows of the trees cast along the road. "You're an angel but don't know it," I recalled hearing in his own voice in my mind just hours after he passed, not understanding the meaning at the time.

His passing had immersed me in the unseen but felt essence of Life and led to a complete personal and spiritual transformation. With Dad's help, I discovered my soul—our true nature, the part of us all that transcends our physical being. What began as signs, dream visitations, and synchronicities without logical explanation grew to wondrous moments of evidential connection with him in meditative states and eventually connections with loved ones of others. I was graced with mediumship abilities, which I was not ready to accept. "I cannot call myself a medium," was my repeated thought. Connections with Dad were welcomed but the label was not. Like a young bird discovering for the first time she has wings but doesn't trust their innate power, I struggled to brave my newfound gift.

Today was Dad's birthday, and just weeks before the one-year anniversary of his passing on November 1. Nearing the log cabin in which I grew up, I breathed in the beauty of the forests and open fields where deer gathered at sunset. I wondered about the man who now lived in my dad's dream home and if he would allow me to spread Dad's ashes on the trails where he once walked our dog. There couldn't be a more meaningful place to honor him. Autumn was his favorite season, and the leaves were preparing to surrender to nature's cycle.

Pulling into my childhood home, I felt nervous and content. A man came out of the house before I could climb the stairs of the wrap-around deck where Dad and I would sit in silence at night, looking up at the stars.

"Hi, there," I yelled from afar as he looked at me quizzically. I walked across the stone driveway to meet him. "My name is Amber and I used to live here. You bought this home from my dad." He introduced himself as Larry and I told him of my wishes and spoke of Dad's love for nature, wildlife, and his log home. Larry shared that he had owned and sold a hunting and fishing store in town, but didn't know my dad.

Larry added, "I've been really lonely the last few years just being here by myself. The house is a lot to care for at my age and the world just seems more depressing every day. But I'd love to help you honor your dad."

With Larry's blessing, my mom, son, and I took the two-track trail from the backyard. My son used a bird call his grandfather had given him and brought in four birds while we spread the ashes around a growing baby pine tree. I knew Dad was there, treasuring the beautiful memory made. I thanked Larry in my heart and hoped he would find happiness again.

The next morning, I sat for daily meditation and the peace that arises within when we bring our full presence to our heart, setting the thoughts and story of who we are aside. In this state of awareness, I suddenly felt the presence of a man and an elderly woman. Without logical explanation, I knew this was Larry's brother and mother. I paused to find paper, feeling I should write everything down.

His brother placed the image of a bird in a box in my mind. I felt pinching at my stomach and knew he had daily injections. I felt he was a teacher, and next he shared the image of building snowmen with his brother and the emotion of fondness. "Thank you," were words I heard as he exited my awareness while his mother's presence returned.

She shared her love of daily walks and mailbox flowers, and showed me in my mind a white kitchen pot holder adorned with a green and yellow flower. I knew it was special and passed down from family. She expressed her appreciation for her son having taken care of her.

I opened my eyes and read what I wrote on the paper. It felt like a mandate to tell Larry, but how could I? "I cannot drive there and tell him I believe I connected with his deceased family!" I yelled aloud. "This is entirely unlike me and could be intrusive to Larry's privacy," the thoughts continued. But that flutter in the gut said this was needed for Larry and a larger purpose I didn't yet understand. I devised a plan that felt authentic and ethical yet scared me immensely.

"This man is going to be the least woo-woo person ever," I said aloud while the sound of stones crunched under my tires in his driveway. Before my fears could turn the car around, Larry came out of the house. Opening the car door, I noticed a small wooden cross in the yard. "Hi Larry! Sorry to bother you again," I said as he walked toward me. "I see that marker in your yard. Did you have a dog? We had a chocolate lab named Thunder."

Larry paused and looked at me with a half-smile and timid expression. He must have decided I felt safe and shared, "My brother lived with me for a while and loved hummingbirds. One flew into the window one day and died. It's silly, but he was so upset and wanted to bury it. We made that marker together."

I looked down at my paper. "Special bird in a box" was the first thing written. Now it was me who felt safe. I told Larry about the past year of afterlife connections with my dad and the occasional connections with others too. But I couldn't say "medium." Larry didn't say a word in return, and I wondered if he thought I was crazy or was simply taking it all in.

"I think I experienced a connection this morning, Larry, with two people who love you: your mother and brother. It's all written on this paper. Would you like to see it?" I held out the page. He didn't speak but took the paper and I waited in silence while he read. Larry looked up from the notes and met my eyes.

"My brother was a history teacher, and I took care of him later in his life. He gave himself injections for diabetes. Mom loved her daily walks, even at ninety-five. She was the only person allowed to get the mail, so she could walk to the mailbox every day. I took care of her until she died."

"I'll be right back," he said, going into the house. He returned holding in his hand a white kitchen pot holder adorned with a green and yellow flower, exactly what I wrote on the paper. "Her dad handmade this for her," he shared. "I had to dig through boxes in the basement to find it. You could have never possibly known about this."

"Oh, this is beautiful, Larry! Both your mother and brother expressed great love and appreciation of you for caring for them," I stated.

Larry asked for my phone number, not sure what to make of this event. One week later, I received his call. "Amber, it's Larry, and I've thought all week about what happened. I want to ask, 'Why did this happen to me?'" Without hesitation I answered, "Larry, I love this because for a year I asked myself this very question, 'Why me?'" The reason is the same. Because you are worthy. We all are."

After a period of silence, Larry shared, "You have a real gift and helped me more than you know. I was so depressed before this and now I have some hope. This has changed my outlook on life." We hung up the phone and purpose swelled within me along with tears. "I'm a medium and I have to accept this," I said aloud. And with that, I braved my wings.

The essence of Life teaches us we are all connected by one big web stitched by love, and woven from Spirit with care. It displays miracles in moments of grief and joy alike. Why? Because we are worthy. Each and every one.

Reflection

What have you learned from a moment of bravery in your life, taking action even in the midst of fear?

How might you or others benefit by letting your own innate gifts shine?

How do you allow and experience divine connection in your life?

Bashert

AMY LINDNER-LESSER

What do two social workers, Lansdowne, Pennsylvania, Lenox, Massachusetts, and October 8 have to do with divine synchronicities?

In January of 1993, my husband Steve and I were raising our two daughters in a suburb of Philadelphia. We were both social workers, involved in our community, and in our children's school. We had a busy life that included a group of families of adopted children like ours, a historic preservation group, and a group to restore our local theatre, along with hosting progressive dinners and house tours.

Steve was unhappy in his job as a supervisor for a community mental health clinic because his time was spent writing case notes and reading his supervisee's notes. I was working as the director of geriatric services for a large hospital system. I loved everything about it— except for the one-hour commute on good days.

What Steve did enjoy was working on our home, and we had recently renovated its exterior. Steve removed all the asphalt shingles and singlehandedly cut saw-toothed shingles to replicate the ones we found hidden under the asphalt. We hired John Crosby Freeman, a colorist who designed the historic paint palettes for

Sherwin Williams Paints, to help us devise a historically appropriate color scheme for our early 1900s American foursquare home. We chose Rookwood Red, Rookwood Green, and a few others.

Our love for Victorian architecture, coupled with our frequent trips to Cape May, New Jersey, where we stayed in bed and breakfasts, weighed heavily in every talk we had about our future. Our plan was to open a bed and breakfast when our daughters left for college. And then life smacked us right in the face.

My mother-in-law died unexpectedly in January 1995. Being an only child, Steve received the entire estate. Within the year, Steve was diagnosed with melanoma, and I with diabetes. We realized the future was not guaranteed, so we took a leap of faith and decided to use his inheritance money to move toward our dream.

Steve quit his job and enrolled in a hotel management program at The Restaurant School in Philadelphia. We researched how to open a bed and breakfast, took several "How to Run a B&B" courses, and thought about where we wanted to live.

We knew we wanted to be close to our family in New York City, but we knew we didn't want our B&B there. Our daughters, being Mexican by birth, are not white. We knew we needed to be in a racially tolerant area. Other considerations for us were our religion, our occupations, our politically and socially liberal values, and that we didn't want to be in an urban or rural area. We needed a location with excellent public schools, interesting things to do in the area, and a culturally enriched community. The Northeast became our clear choice.

While Steve studied, I researched. We visited many bed and breakfasts, and properties we believed could be turned into one. By the time we'd finished our final course, our dream was taking shape: buy an existing property, without a restaurant, with at least twelve rooms, employees to do some of the work and free us for time with each other and our children, in an area with other existing inns, and in an area where we wanted to live and raise our children.

We came close to purchasing an inn in Vermont that had a restaurant until we realized what an obstacle that created. Steve would have to wake up early in the morning to cook breakfast, prep dinner in the afternoons, and then cook all evening until late in the night. I would be responsible for almost all childcare and checking guests in and out. We would be ships passing in the night. No way!

In June 1996, our friend and partner in our inn broker team called about two inns for sale. One was in the Northeast Kingdom area of Vermont, and I vetoed that immediately due to its rural location and because it had a restaurant. The other was in the Berkshires of Western Massachusetts.

Here's where the synchronicities really begin. She told me the name of the inn was The Wookwood. I remember thinking, "What an unusual name." I realized that with her German accent, she was saying Rookwood. Remember the colors our house was painted? Rookwood Red and Green! Both Steve and I had gone to sleepaway camps in the Berkshires, a fact we discovered on one of our trips to see the inn in Vermont, where we ended up staying in an inn in Cummington, MA. Steve's camp became that inn, while my camp was in the next town, West Cummington. More synchronicities.

We went up to see The Rookwood in July and spent the night with my mother, who was renting a house with a friend about a mile away. It was love at first sight! The inn was a beautiful Queen Anne with two turrets, twenty guest rooms, each with its own bathroom, and a beautiful streetscape. The address was 11 Old Stockbridge Road, and it received mail at post office box 1717; our house in PA was 117.

James Taylor has always been my favorite singer, and all I could think about was his lullaby, "Sweet Baby James," in which he sings, "the Berkshires seemed dream-like … from Stockbridge to Boston." I was sold! As we walked around, I could envision our antiques filling the rooms, Steve cooking breakfast, and us living in this inn. We saw ourselves going to Tanglewood, as we had as kids, only this time bringing our daughters to hear the Boston Symphony, going to plays at Shakespeare & Company, and enjoying the rest of the cultural venues and museums, as well as hiking in the Berkshire Hills.

After a few months of negotiations and inspections, on October 8, 1996, The Rookwood Inn became ours. That day would have been my mother-in-law's seventy-fifth birthday. There's a word in Yiddish: bashert. It means, meant to be or destined. That's how this felt.

My best friend Liz had come with us to keep our daughters occupied while we were busy with the closing. She had lived in the Berkshires for a few years and told us that the former owner of The Rookwood (then the Quincy Lodge), also Jewish, had given talks in the local high schools about his Holocaust experience. As well, his son and our daughters went to the same camp in the Poconos, although many years apart.

Steve's melanoma returned in January 1996. He died a mere two-and-a-half years after we bought the inn.

I believe the universe was telling us we made the right decision, at the right time. We never know what the future will bring. I learned not to put life off—to live fully in the present.

During my time at the inn, I became a justice of the peace and performed many weddings there and in the area. At one wedding, James Taylor was a guest. He came up to me afterward to tell me I did a great job. I told him that my first ever concert was when he opened for Carole King at Madison Square Garden, and I had seen him in concert every year since.

I owned the inn for about twenty-three years after Steve died, raising both our daughters there. At the beginning of December 2020, I hosted and participated in a retreat that included strategic meditation. I saw myself in a square somewhere in Mexico. I remember sharing the journey with the others and saying it was great but wouldn't happen as I had responsibilities at the inn.

Two weeks later, right before Christmas, a man rang the bell and asked if I wanted to sell. It hadn't crossed my mind, but the voice in my head reminded me, "Every business is for sale at the right price." Three months later, the inn had new owners.

The universe works in mysterious ways. My entire twenty-five-year inn career was filled with divine synchronicities: the name of the inn and our paint colors, moving from Pennsylvania to Massachusetts, taking over on Shirley's seventy-fifth birthday, and so many more. I just needed to keep my eyes and mind open to see them. Thank you, universe, I am grateful for each of these and those yet to come.

Reflection

When in your life have you been guided to make a radical shift in where you lived, where you worked, and how you showed up in your life? What happened?

Think of a celebrity you admire. How would it feel to have them say they admired you? Under what circumstances could that happen?

When have you or a loved one received a medical diagnosis that shifted the way you looked at your life? What changed?

Embracing that I'm a Teacher
ROBIN FITZSIMONS

I again pulled the "Spiritual Teacher" card from the Life Purpose Oracle Card deck. But *I'm NOT a teacher*!

In 2012, I found myself entrenched in a job that had lost its luster. Initially, diving into graphic design filled me with excitement. Still, as time wore on, the mounting stress of deadlines, the suffocating toxicity of the workplace, and the overall oppressive atmosphere began to take their toll. Each morning, I'd embark on my commute with a hopeful mantra, "Today is going to be a good day," only to have my optimism shattered the moment I stepped through the office doors. It was as if an invisible force had seized control of my being, and I was not my best self. The prospect of returning to that stifling environment grew increasingly daunting each day.

Picture this: A rustic campground, the sounds of nature, and the enticing aroma of freshly prepared food drifting through the air. As my husband and I visited my parents during their camping trip, we stumbled upon a woman sampling an array of mouthwatering foods on a picnic table. My husband, never one to shy away from new experiences, eagerly dove in, urging me to join him.

"Try this," he insisted. "It's right up your alley!"

And he was right—the flavors danced on my palate, leaving me craving more.

What we sampled was made from a lineup of all-natural, preservative-free spice blends from a new multi-level marketing (MLM) company. Although initially hesitant about joining, my curiosity got the best of me. With a simple sign-up and kit purchase, I was thrust into a whirlwind of unexpected opportunities. Soon after, I received a call from my upline urging me to host two launch parties. Despite my reservations, I took the plunge.

To my surprise, the response was overwhelming. People were eager to experience the magic of these spice blends, and before I knew it, I had three eager recruits signed up under me. Without even trying, I had inadvertently kickstarted my journey as a team leader in the world of MLM. And so began my adventure with Wildtree, a journey filled with unexpected twists and turns but ultimately leading me down a path of growth and success.

As an introvert and empath, the mere thought of hosting a party filled me with dread. With each drive to an event, I secretly hoped for a low turnout—hardly the ideal scenario for someone trying to make sales! But then something remarkable happened. As I delved deeper into understanding and utilizing the products, a newfound confidence began to bloom within me. Suddenly, the prospect of showcasing these products became less daunting, and my anxiety dissipated. And to top it all off, the additional income was a delightful perk that sweetened the deal even further!

My job was getting increasingly stressful, and I knew something was coming. I began clearing out my desk, preparing myself for the possibility of being let go from the company where I had dedicated over two decades of my life. However, fate had other plans in store for me. Just when I thought the axe was about to fall, I received news that turned my world upside down: I was *promoted*! My income became salaried instead of working hourly (with many overtime hours)! You do the math!

Amidst the chaos of my professional life, I found solace and respite in my Wildtree parties. Little did I know, these gatherings were more than just a temporary escape—they were quietly shaping and preparing me for the challenges and opportunities ahead.

Faced with the daunting prospect of leaving behind the security of my full-time corporate job, I grappled with many reasons why breaking free seemed impossible. As I sat and wrote down these obstacles—the steady income, the invaluable health insurance, the looming worry of loan repayments, and more—I couldn't help but feel overwhelmed by the weight of my circumstances. Each item on the list seemed to reinforce that escape was a distant dream, forever out of reach.

But amidst the despair, a glimmer of hope emerged—a flicker of possibility that refused to be extinguished. With a resolve born of necessity, I made a pivotal decision: if I couldn't break free from the corporate grind, I could at least carve out a space on the side, pursuing a passion that had long stirred my soul. Inspired by my love for health and fitness, I seized the opportunity to channel the extra income from my Wildtree ventures into a new direction: enrolling in the Health Coaching program at the Institute for Integrative Nutrition.

As I embarked on this transformative journey, I found solace and camaraderie in the company of fellow Wildtree enthusiasts who shared my vision for a brighter, more fulfilling future. Together, we navigated the challenges and triumphs of our dual pursuits, each step bringing us closer to realizing our deepest aspirations.

I'll never forget the day I sat down with my notebook, pouring my heart out to my guides and angels. I pleaded for clarity on when and how to break free from my corporate chains and begged for the courage to embrace a new journey. Fast forward two weeks, and I found myself handing in my resignation. It was like some unseen force had taken over, propelling me into the unknown. The week prior, I stumbled upon a space for rent, deciding to check it out on a whim. Little did I know that a spontaneous visit would lead to the birth of Robin's Center for Wellness just a month later. With no clients and uncertainty looming over every step, I embarked on this adventure with unwavering trust in the universe.

About a month into my entrepreneurial journey, I encountered a fellow health coach on social media. We decided to grab lunch and chat about our respective paths. What was meant to be a short meet-up turned into four hours. As I left her office, I found myself holding a Reiki manual and an attunement that would unlock a whole new world of healing. It was as if the universe was nudging me towards my next step.

A month later, an unexpected pop-up ad appeared on my computer screen despite my trusty pop-up blocker. It advertised an Angel Reader's Certification course, and without hesitation, I signed up. Suddenly, Reiki and Angel Readings became integral parts of my service offerings. It was as if the puzzle pieces were falling into place, one by one.

Soon after, opportunities began knocking at my door. A massage therapist expressed interest in renting space in my center. At the same time, teachers reached out about offering classes on Akashic Records—a skill I acquired because of this and would later utilize. These ventures helped cover the rent and added depth to my services.

Little did I know, this was just the beginning. As I delved deeper into the realm of healing, I discovered the power of Past Life Healing sessions. This modality seamlessly integrated into my practice, enriching my clients' experiences in ways I never imagined.

Amidst the chaos, I found solace in oracle cards, seeking guidance not just for others but for myself, too. Ironically, the "Spiritual Teacher" card kept surfacing, but I brushed it off, insisting, "I am not a teacher." Yet, as my intuition blossomed, my social circle transformed, and serendipitous events unfolded, I realized that everything led me toward becoming a spiritual teacher. In each session—whether coaching, reading, or practicing Reiki—I unwittingly imparted knowledge, offering people something tangible to take with them. Eventually, I embraced this role, delving into teaching Reiki and other spiritual classes and, in the past year, even venturing into online Zoom and self-study courses.

As an introvert, I was never one to seek out the spotlight. Growing up, I shied away from speaking in front of groups, preferring the comfort of solitude. But then came Wildtree—a turning point that transformed my apprehension into empowerment. Reflecting on my journey, each twist and turn, every challenge and triumph, contributed to the grand mosaic of my life's path. Transforming worries and fears into unwavering trust was the key that unlocked the door to my current role as a spiritual coach, mentor, healer, and, yes—unexpectedly, a teacher.

Reflection

How did the unexpected loss of a job or a partner impact your personal growth?

What role did overcoming initial hesitations and stepping out of comfort zones play in your journey?

In what ways have seemingly unrelated ventures contribute to your development of confidence and resilience?

A Big Loving Shove Toward Destiny

LISA HROMADA

My heart raced as I ran through Heathrow airport, darting between other travelers. My flight from Paris had been delayed, causing me to miss my connecting flight in London. Finding an unusual humor in the challenge, I smiled and quietly chanted to myself in a breathless whisper, "I'm going to make it!" I was determined to catch the last flight of the night heading home to the States.

I wasn't expecting to stay long in London, so I didn't carry currency, and I didn't own a credit card or a phone. With all my belongings still on the plane from Paris, if I didn't hurry, I'd be stranded for the night without food, a place to stay, or a way of contacting my family back home. That was the summer just after I turned twenty years old — a time in my life when I was just beginning to discover what it meant to be on my own, trying to figure out my future.

My confidence in the uncertainty of getting home that night was unlike who I'd known myself to be before spending the summer alone traveling Paris and the south of France. I wouldn't call myself "adventurous." I prefer certainty, security, and comfort. I had my group of friends, a daily routine, and a fresh start in college.

I'd been in a long-distance relationship for a couple of years with a boy who lived in another part of Europe, and that summer I'd planned to visit him, first making a quick stop through Paris. Despite my plans, in the weeks prior to leaving, he ended the relationship. Rather than canceling my trip and losing money, I decided to stay in Paris. It was as if the Universe was giving me a big, loving shove to be on my own, for a reason that I did not yet know.

The Universe had plans for me. Those plans included being separated from everything I'd known and who I thought I was so that I could see what was possible and set the stage for the life that was divinely planned for me when I returned. Unbeknownst to me then, the Universe was about to send me on a profound journey of self-discovery. Traveling alone — taking planes, trains, metros, and a few crazy-fast Paris taxi rides — with no smartphone to translate the language, connect me with family and friends, or give me a GPS of where to go and how to navigate the way, I had to rely on myself for the first time in my life.

It's no mistake that the Universe sent me to Paris with only a tourist map, a pocket travel French-English dictionary, and a film camera. Life has a funny way of showing you what you're made of. All my life, I lacked confidence and self-trust. But now, I'd be required to cultivate it. I would often be called to trust myself and find my certainty, security, and comfort.

My travels through Paris involved nearly being stranded a few times, spending an afternoon in a police station to report a break-in to an officer who knew no English, and many other adventurous and uncomfortable moments. It was also filled with a few surprising joyful encounters, beautiful art and landmarks, and a chance to go inward and reflect on the bigger picture of why I was there, what I really wanted in my life, what mattered most, and what possibilities and potential were meant for me next.

There's something magical that happens when you're alone, with no distractions and detached from the story of who you've believed yourself to be or who others have told you that you are. In these still moments, you begin to see who you are beyond your life experiences. You discover what you want. You get a glimpse of a higher version of yourself you didn't know existed. That was my experience in the quiet moments while staying in a tiny town in the south of France.

After a few weeks of exploring Paris, I was invited to go on holiday to Laissac. While there, although welcomed with open arms, I often felt uncomfortable. I secluded myself in a small room of the family house where I was staying, looking out the window and journaling. The laughter of the children downstairs running around and the humming of three or more conversations happening simultaneously between the adults echoed through the door. Despite the happy activity and lively banter surrounding me, I felt lonely, heartbroken, and isolated from the familiarity of home.

Despite having studied the French language for six years, I didn't understand the French dialect used in that area of France, which led me to feel further isolated. But I soon realized that was exactly what I needed. Looking out the window framed with charming bay shutters, I viewed beautiful grassy hills and a quaint cobblestone town. In the distance, at the top of a high hill, stood the cross of a church. At first, the church didn't hold much significance, although I was drawn to its presence. It stood tall and prominent — a symbol of love, renewal, and the promise of something better. I often stared at it in tears, asking for guidance and answers. That's when the words came, and I began to journal.

"I see that you are hurting," I wrote. *"It seems that you have forgotten who you are. (Here is a reminder: You are 'love'.) I see you longing for what you once had. The comfort of something familiar, or relief from a broken heart."* My hand moved steadily as the words formed. As

I continued to write, I could feel my stress and sadness ease. I was no longer alone.

"*You used to laugh,*" I continued. "*I can still hear the sound of your laughter, and I can still see the light your body produces as you let off this vibrant, warm energy.*" I had forgotten what it felt like to laugh—to be lighthearted. I had been so preoccupied with my thoughts and unhappy feelings. As I continued to write, I felt a knowing arise within me. It was a realization that no matter how alone, hopeless, or defeated I might feel, I am always in a loving presence.

"*I don't know if you can see me, but I am right before you, looking into your eyes. Your thoughts blind you from seeing my presence. But I can see straight to your heart. Your lips don't move, but I hear you. You feel alone, but you need not feel that way. You fear that things won't get better, but they will. Know that there is always a way to happiness, but you will not find it outside of yourself. In the pursuit of truth, you must not let those about you divert you from your path but let them give you a reason why to keep moving forward. Beauty exists in the stillness of each moment. Accepting the tears, should they come. Surrendering to the momentary emptiness you may feel. Acknowledging sadness as it passes through you. In this stillness, you can allow any struggle to dissolve into an invisible presence of love.*"

Little did I know then, but these words hinted at the work I'd be led to do over a decade later. After a week in Laissac, I eagerly returned to Paris. I spent my remaining weeks there welcoming old friends traveling through, sharing laughs, stories of our travels, memories, and visions for a future that I felt was clearer and I was more confident about. And then, as a sacred, symbolic close to an epic trip was that moment in the Heathrow airport, confidently determined to get the last flight out.

Out of breath, I reached the airport kiosk and booked a last-minute flight to a city two hours outside my hometown. Once finally home, after an impromptu stay in Paris sparked by the ending of a relationship and along the way discovering myself, what happened next would prove how divinely synchronistic the Universe works.

Within a few months after coming back, I met my husband. Over two decades and two incredible kids later, we continue to grow and evolve as a family. It's been my truth that sometimes life requires you to take a step away from the familiarity of everyday life and who you've been so that you can discover a more profound truth of who you are, who you want to be, and a higher potential that you don't yet know is there. The discoveries you make through your challenges often lead you to the destinies meant for you all along.

Reflection

What opportunities are available to you through your challenges?

What is life calling you to do or be through your challenges, delays, or detours in life?

What's possible for you when you're clear on what matters most to you?

The Divine Hand Leads Me Home

BONNIE SNYDER

When we first visited the west coast of Florida, my daughter was a few months old, just tiny enough to sleep in a drawer. We traveled from Orlando to the west coast to enjoy the highlight of our summer. How wonderful to be swimming in the clear, calm, blue waters, relaxing with a book, and watching the stunningly colorful sunsets. Although I couldn't see how it could happen, I started to dream of living on Florida's west coast.

Looking back, I can trace the divine hand at work.

It wasn't until both my kids were in college that I got an invisible tap on my shoulder. In October of that year, I heard, "It's time to move, to move on." I wasn't emotionally ready. I didn't want to leave. I had lived in Orlando my whole adult life! I would be leaving everyone and everything I knew. I couldn't go to the store without seeing someone I knew. I was comfortable there.

I had my counseling and coaching practice, and my husband had his business. But soon I noticed I had more empty slots. My husband changed the focus of his practice. Money was tight. How could we make this big move?

By January, the signs were evident. My schedule had holes like Swiss cheese. I knew that with my focus on coaching and my husband's new efforts for his business, our work was portable.

To soothe our financial concerns, my husband applied for a part-time job on the west coast —and got it! This was when the transition and magic started. As luck would have it, the job was to start in two weeks. Yikes! How could we do that?

Through divine intervention (or was it magic?), we found an apartment that was available to rent immediately. Days later, we were moving just enough furniture into the apartment for my husband to feel comfortable.

I will never forget the drive across the Tampa Bay Causeway from the mainland to the beach side. The fog was dense and thick, like milky cotton, and we couldn't even see the car in front of us. "This fog is a metaphor," I told my husband. "We have no idea how this is all going to unfold." As we reached the beach side, rays of sun pushed their way through the clouds, so bright I had to put on my sunglasses.

The view from his new apartment was spectacular. Smelling the salt air and seeing the beautiful shimmering water was refreshing and promising; I could feel my heart lift.

We signed a one-year lease. We weren't sure how the house was going to sell or how long the transition would take for me to move with the rest of our belongings. Uncertain and nervous, we were hoping for the best.

The house went up for sale in February and sold within ten days. I had thirty days to pack everything up. It was overwhelming, and both emotionally and physically tiring. I was alone, packing between patients, telling them I was moving, and saying farewell to friends and years of a life I loved. There were lots of tears.

The apartment would be a tight fit for two. Since we didn't yet know where we wanted to settle, we decided to rent a house. There were two communities, East Lake and Safety Harbor, where we thought we might fit. The first time we checked the ads, we saw a house in East Lake.

It was perfect. Situated next to a wooded park with walking trails, I could walk every day in nature. And there was a nearby YMCA for my gym-going husband to join.

This seemed too good to be true, but we had the lease on the apartment to consider. Divine synchronicity again—the landlord at the apartment agreed to a sublease. The weekend we advertised the apartment, a woman subleased it for the rest of the year.

The rental house was small, but we had sold most of our furniture and the rest was in storage. It was a freeing time as we didn't have the responsibility of caring for our own home.

In the fall, we started our search and fell in love with a house. I bought an afghan with colors that matched the master bedroom. I thought this would be a positive sign, symbolic of moving into our new home. We were buying the home without a realtor, and the house sold before we placed the offer. Holding the afghan made me feel like I had failed in creating what I wanted. All the synchronicities that had happened faded away into a river of disappointed tears.

It was time to find a realtor to help with our search. But who?

Meeting new people wasn't easy. I worked from a home office now, so had no office friends and had moved from 100 miles away. Tampa Bay was like a foreign country. We didn't have a dog or kids to easily open doors to conversations and new friendships. I had, however, joined several networking groups.

At one group, I met and hit it off with Judy, who had a great sense of humor and also happened to be a realtor. I introduced her to Mary, the one person my husband and I already knew in this area. I suggested we start a mastermind group. My husband, Mary, Judy, and I got together each week to work on our businesses. This filled my heart with much-needed companionship.

Over a period of a few months, Judy and I looked at houses on weekends—so many that my head spun. Only two homes we saw were even close to what I was looking for. I was deeply discouraged. I had not made many new friends, so I loved the lunches and occasional shopping Judy and I did together after trudging through houses. It was a welcome perk with good conversation and laughter.

After months of house hunting, I went into a tunnel of dark desperation, thinking we would never find a house. Judy told me to focus on my non-negotiables. I felt I would never find someplace quiet, where nature was my back-door neighbor. Our rental house was noisy with traffic that sounded like a speedway. I couldn't open the windows or sit outside and have a conversation. The noise was like poison to my system.

Despite being discouraged, I created a vision board with pictures and words that represented the feelings we wanted in a new home. One picture showed a trellis with jasmine to represent a garden. Another was the view from a home's upstairs loft, looking down over a lovely living area.

During this time, my friend Lisa from New Jersey was looking to move to Florida, and she sent me the listing for a home she was interested in. One day while driving, I realized that the neighborhood she was looking at was just down the road from us. What a coincidence!

Around the same time, my networking group was looking for a speaker. Through my referral, Lisa was chosen to be the keynote speaker for the event. By this time, Lisa's plans had changed, and she had decided not to move. While she was in town, she asked if Judy would take us to the house she had been interested in.

I had seen the listing in my email but had never opened it or considered it, since it was a larger home than what we were looking for.

As I walked in the door, I saw the sunlight shining on the leaves of trees hugging the pool area, the stunning purple color of the orchids on a bench, and the sun sparkling on the water in the pool. I immediately felt a sense of peace.

As we walked upstairs, I realized I had missed living in a two-story home. I noted the view from the overlook opened down into a great family room. Then, as we walked outside, there it was: a white trellis with white jasmine blooming. Instantly, I knew this was to be our next home.

When we align with something and move into the flow, if we are taken off track, the hand of the divine guides us back on course. I realized that once we made the decision to move, the divine hand was guiding us all the way with every synchronicity!

Reflection

How can remembering synchronicities from the past support you in creating something new in your life?

Is there a time in your life when you *let go* or surrendered worrying about something, and you magically found synchronicities that led you to what you thought would never happen?

How are miracles, magic, and synchronicities connected?

How I Became a Radio Psychic

SHA BLACKBURN

I have been psychic for as long as I can remember. When I was less than ten years old, I only used my intuition and the voice of my soul to speak my "wisdom." And when I turned twelve, an older neighbor from up the street gave me the Gypsy Witch Fortune Telling Cards because she thought I would get a kick out of them. I sure did! I progressed to the tarot in my mid-teens and began a more earnest career through my late high school and college years. My belief in my psychic abilities rarely wavered; they always seemed part of who I am.

When I became a mom at twenty-three, my husband was not thrilled with my psychic–witchy self and I put this part of myself on the back burner of my life for a few years. But when we split, I realized I had to raise my son alone. I needed a side hustle to shore up my income—something I could do at my own pace and when I was available. That's why I returned to psychic fairs and working out of little new-age shops.

As I dove back into leveraging my psychic abilities, I met a man who worked at one of the shops where I did readings, and we became the very best of friends, having breakfast every Saturday morning, sharing secrets and gossip kind of dear friends. He later opened his own business and began advertising on a local radio station.

One day in 2004, I got an early morning panicked phone call from my friend. His truck had broken down, and he had an appointment that he needed to be at for 8 am. I happened to have that day off and could give him a ride. I never asked where he was going; he just provided directions as I drove. As we approached our destination in the tiny harbor town above Cape Cod, we pulled into a meager plaza that had clearly seen better days. The center hosted a collection of random businesses: a coffee shop, a daycare, a radio station office, and a liquor store. Quite the odd combination of places! We pulled into the plaza when he announced that he was scheduled to do readings on live radio! *How interesting!* I felt excited for him to have that opportunity.

"Come in with me. I'll introduce you to the radio DJs," he said. So, I did.

We entered the studio's waiting area, which smelled oddly sterile. A Dutch door stood at the far end, it's upper half open, while the closed lower portion kept visitors from walking into the station's inner sanctum of offices and sound rooms. I later learned that the top portion would be locked after hours. It felt as if the walls absorbed sound making the are almost eerily quiet. The on-air personalities came out to greet us.

My friend introduced me as "The LoonWitch," my stage name. One of the DJs asked, "Do you also read tarot?"

"I do," I said.

"Would you consider joining us on-air to do some readings?"

Those who know me well would say that I am sometimes reserved. My heart pounded. *Me? On live radio?* All of my readings until then had been in person. I didn't know how it would work to do a reading for someone over the phone…not to mention being LIVE on the radio! My friend eagerly agreed on my behalf. And there I was: walking into a tiny radio sound studio with acoustic tiling on the wall, a huge control panel, and barely enough room to walk through to take my seat on a stool.

There were three stations for the DJ's and guests to sit at, each with is own headset and microphone. Once we had our headphones on, and the microphones were adjusted, it was my turn to be introduced to the vast network of listeners on a Friday morning FM drive-time show.

I always have my tarot deck with me. They are my dearest friends, and I often consult them when I need guidance and support. I had quietly pulled a card for myself when we first entered the broadcast studio to bolster my courage—or find out if I should run for the hills. The card I pulled was the major arcana card, "The High Priestess." The High Priestess represents the power, the higher self, and the guide who knows your secrets and knows only to answer the questions asked. She is a very spiritual and intuitive being. I felt buoyed by receiving her as the answer to my question. With newfound confidence, I realized I could give live readings on the radio.

My first experience of reading on live radio was terrifying and exhilarating all at the same time. The first reading I did made the caller cry happy tears. I don't remember the question she asked, but I remember her reaction to my response—and how everyone in the radio studio fell silent as if awestruck by my accuracy. I felt impressed by myself as well!

As a practice, I go into every reading with no expectations other than the client will receive the information that they need, even if it's not the information that they want. When I can provide clear and specific information for my client with precision and accuracy, it's always a thrill! It's like a pat on my back from the Universe, reminding me that my gifts are something beautiful that I should keep sharing.

At the end of that first show, I was invited back.

I continued being a guest on that show for twelve years for one Friday morning a month. And since then, I have been a guest reader on multiple radio shows and podcasts. As of this writing,

I have built a thriving business as a psychic and spiritual coach with clients in nineteen countries around the world.

Who knew that helping a friend in a moment of need would lead to not only one interesting experience, and also an amazing opportunity to really create an amazing life! When opportunity knocks, remember to say, "Yes!"

Reflection

In what ways have your introversion tendencies played into you staying small? What changed when you embraced who you are?

What dreams do you secretly have and how can you manifest having them come true? What would be your first step?

When have you used tools like Oracle Cards to guide your decision-making process? What is helpful about using such tools?

Editor's Note

DEBORAH KEVIN

Welcome to *Divine Synchronicity: Women's Stories of Magic, Miracles & Manifesting*, an anthology that weaves together the ethereal threads of life's most magical moments. As the editor-in-chief of this collection, I am honored to present stories that illuminate the divine synchronicities that have profoundly shaped the lives of the women featured in these pages.

Divine Synchronicity resonates deeply with me, as my own journey has been marked by extraordinary encounters that defy mere coincidence. One of the most transformative experiences in my life was meeting a remarkable woman who helped me realize my dream of walking the Camino de Santiago, an ancient pilgrimage that culminates in Santiago, Spain. This profound journey not only fulfilled a personal aspiration but also connected me with my soul's purpose in ways I could never have anticipated.

Another remarkable synchronicity was reconnecting with the love of my life after thirty-one years. This reunion, filled with wonder and joy, is a testament to the universe's divine timing and the invisible threads that bind our destinies. These experiences, among many others, have instilled in me an unwavering belief in the power of divine synchronicity.

A NOTE FROM THE EDITOR

Divine Synchronicity acts as a celestial guide, urging us to ascend to the essence of our highest selves. It calls us to heed the whispers of our soul, make courageous decisions, and birth ideas and creations touched by the divine. It invites us to dive deep within, emerging with a profound understanding of who we are and the boundless love that sustains us.

In this anthology, you will find stories of women who have experienced divine synchronicities, moments where magic and mystery unfolded as they paid attention to the signs around them. These stories celebrate the endless capacity for everyday miracles and the divine's role in shaping our journeys. By reading these stories, you will become part of this larger narrative, connected by the influence of the divine in our lives.

May you be inspired to recognize and embrace the divine synchronicities in your own life. These moments are not mere coincidences, but powerful tools for your spiritual growth. By acknowledging and embracing them, you take control of your journey and are guided towards your highest path.

Deborah Kevin
Managing Editor

About Our Authors

SHA BLACKBURN

Sha Blackburn is an internationally known psychic. She is known to be compassionate, insightful, and "scary accurate." She is passionate about life and helping others to learn, understand, and cope. Sha has been featured on AM, FM, and internet radio since 2003, offering her gifts. She uses her motivation, healing, and psychic abilities to help people transform their lives. Sha was named "Woman of the Year in 2012," by the NAPW, and was named "Inspirational Woman of the Year in 2014" by WRN1 Radio. You can learn more about her at www.LoonWitch.com.

ABOUT OUR AUTHORS

DONNA BURGHER

As a Dream Catalyst mentor, Radiant Mindset coach, and host of the Faith-Inspired Living podcast, **Donna Burgher** specializes in guiding you to live a faith-inspired life. Through private coaching and group programs, Donna merges practical tools and biblical principles to help you activate joy, cultivate a positive mindset, amplify your gratitude, and partner with God to co-create your Divinely-Designed Dreams™ so you can live a happy and blessed life filled with joy, passion, and purpose. Learn more at www.DonnaBurgher.com.

LAURIE BURKHALTER

Laurie Burkhalter, a certified Reiki advanced crystal master and creation team coach, is passionate about holistic health and wellness, shamanic astrology, crystals and crystal healing, spiritual development and growth, healing self and soul, and elemental oracle cards. She sells crystals in her online store to support those who want healing for themselves and their loved ones. Learn more at: www.LaurieBurkhalter.com.

CRYSTAL COCKERHAM

Crystal Cockerham, spiritual mentor, feminine wisdom teacher, and author, works with empathic women to deepen their relationship with the Divine, learn their souls' language, and hone their empathic gifts so they can create the divinely inspired life they envision, desire, and deserve. Crystal works with women in a sacred circle setting as well as individually both virtually and in person through spiritual and transformational retreats, red tents, moon circles, and more! Learn more at www.CrystalCockerham.com.

TYWANAH EVETTE

Tywanah Evette, an intuitive healer and psychic with thirty-five years of business experience, has transitioned into a deeper spiritual realm. She has guided entrepreneurs and even White House appointees, blending intuition and empathy to navigate professional and personal challenges. Tywanah embraces this new chapter as a soulful evolution. Guided by her mother Lorraine, Tywanah offers intuitive healing, psychic insight, mentorship, and spiritual wisdom. She aims to create harmony between material and spiritual realms for personal growth. Learn more at www.BlackButterflyGoddess.com.

ROBIN FITZSIMONS

Robin Fitzsimons, founder of Wellness with Robin in Platteville, WI, is an intuitive, spiritual teacher and healer, certified holistic life coach, Usui Reiki master, Akashic record reader, angel reader, certified assertiveness coach, and certified Silent Counseling practitioner. She's passionate about following her Divine Path and helping people. Robin is a powerful, heart-centered, energy-loving practitioner who can't wait to serve you, whether with an individual session, event, class, or online. She will welcome you with open arms and open hearts. Learn more at www.WellnessWithRobin.com.

JUDY GALLAURESI

Judy Gallauresi is a distinguished mindset and mindfulness mentor, skilled Soul Coaching® practitioner, and oracle card reader. Passionate about guiding clients, she merges wisdom with wit to unlock her clients' inherent potential. Judy's approach encourages clients to trust their intuition and clear physical and mental clutter, facilitating self-discovery and empowerment. She is dedicated to leading her clients toward clarity and joy and unveiling their inner wisdom, making each journey a transformative experience. Learn more at www.CrystalConcepts.com.

SARA GOMEZ

Sara Gomez is a neuro-somatic counselor, writer, and teacher. Trained in somatic trauma therapy, neuropsychology, hypnotherapy, and transpersonal energy healing, she provides evidence-based tools and techniques, and intuitive guidance to empower women to break out of "fight, flight, freeze" patterns and get back in touch with their bodies' innate wisdom. Her passion for this work is witnessing the moment a woman feels safe coming home to herself, and she radiates her unique power and magic. Learn more at www.SaraGomezHealing.com.

LISA HROMADA

Lisa Hromada is an Empowered Lifeview™ guide, spiritual life coach, and creator of Love is the Seed™ — a spirit-led lifework dedicated to helping purpose-driven women breakthrough life challenges, reclaim their inner peace, and cultivate the clarity they need to live a life of meaning, joy, and spiritual connection. Through her Empowered Lifeview™ & Divine Reset™ methodology, Lisa guides women to live at their highest potential and on their higher life path. Learn more at www.LoveIsTheSeed.

ABOUT OUR AUTHORS

DAWN MICHELE JACKSON

As an Advanced Grief Recovery Specialist®, Certified Infinite Possibilities Trainer, women's retreat facilitator, registered nurse, and Amazon bestselling author, **Dawn Michele Jackson**'s primary focus is to guide individuals through healing their hearts, transforming their lives, and rediscovering joy. Driven by a profound mission, she is dedicated to helping individuals uncover their inner light and make the profound shift from surviving to thriving. Dawn skillfully supports her clients to achieve holistic wellness of mind, body, and spirit. Learn more at www.DawnMicheleJackson.com.

WIOLETA KAPUSTA

Wioleta Kapusta, founder of The CEO of Your Life Community, runs "Own Your Worth" challenges and deeper dives with her "Reconnected Woman Experience." Her mission is to inspire amazing women to transform their lives, create deeper connections with themselves and others, and to support them so they can stand in their power, using their voices to make the difference they always wanted to for others and the world. Learn more at www.WioletaKapusta.net.

AMBER KASIC

Amber Kasic is an evidential medium, author, speaker, and former classroom teacher. After a shared death experience with her father in 2020, she began a journey of discovery and connection with our greater reality, guided by her dad in spirit. She shares that journey with audiences worldwide. She now inspires others to explore just what is possible in our lives, as love is limitless, and we are connected beyond our human understanding. It's nature's way.
Learn more at www.NaturesWayOpen.com.

YVETTE LEFLORE

Yvette LeFlore is an intuitive energy healer, Reiki master teacher, and crystal clinician. Yvette's mission is to support people to fill their energetic cups to overflowing so they have enough to give to others without depleting themselves. She offers group and individual healings, Reiki 1–3 classes in person and virtually, and crystal divination. Yvette lives in Salem, Virginia, with her husband and two four-legged healing partners, Jasper and Cleo.
Learn more at www.HealingWithYvette.com.

ABOUT OUR AUTHORS

AMY LINDNER-LESSER

Amy Lindner-Lesser, MSW, an Advanced Grief Recovery Method™ specialist and certified Life Transitions coach, compassionately supports women through the emotions of loss and grief arising from major life transitions. Whether it's heartbreaking grief from the loss of a loved one, disorientation due to the loss of a job or relationship, an identity crisis or health challenge, or other life disruption, Amy passionately guides clients to navigate the transition with self-compassion assisting them to move through grief to growth and into joy. www.INNtrospection.com.

CAROLYN MARIE

Carolyn Marie is a creative catalyst and possibility ignitor for midlife women ready to create their next best chapter of life. Carolyn spent twenty years dedicated to personal study of energy, spiritual, and personal growth modalities she used to transform her life. Carolyn is passionately committed to supporting women in midlife to explore what lights them up, excavate what's holding them back, and to activate their soul's gift to live with purpose, passion and joy. Learn more at www.CarolynMarieCoaching.com.

FELICIA MESSINA-D'HAITI

Felicia Messina-D'Haiti lovingly supports others in clearing physical, mental, emotional, and spiritual blockages to bring greater alignment to their homes and lives. Felicia is a Feng Shui and Soul Coaching® teacher/practitioner. She is a speaker, award-winning educator, and contributing author of several best-selling books. Connect with Felicia at www.FeliciadHaiti.com, receive a complimentary gift, and explore her offerings, including certification courses in feng shui, space clearing, Soul Coaching,® clutter coaching, and Usui Reiki.

NANCY OKEEFE

Nancy OKeefe is a Certified Quantum Human Design Specialist, intuitive business coach, and compassionate transformer who helps women entrepreneurs peel back the layers of who they have been taught to be and how they have been conditioned to do business, so they can live their inner truth and build an abundant and sustainable business that feeds their soul. Learn more at www.NancyOKeefeCoaching.com.

ABOUT OUR AUTHORS

BARB PRITCHARD

Barb Pritchard, founder and creative force of Infinity Brand Design, is a visionary brand strategist and intuitive designer with twenty years of experience. Specializing in an empathy-driven approach, she empowers spiritual entrepreneurs and shapes transformative brands, aligning mission-focused businesses with their soul clients while leveraging deep expertise from her work with Fortune 100 & 500 companies. Barb is also an author, speaker, and advocate for purposeful living, enjoying global travel and cultural exploration. Learn more at www.InfinityBrand.design.

BRENDA REIMER-HARDER

Brenda Reimer-Harder, a certified Reiki/Chakra and energy therapy practitioner, is an author and proud mom of three point-five young adults. She worked as a non-certified professional accountant in the corporate world for thirty-five years before she became a certified holistic wellness coach and soul coaching card reader. Brenda enhanced her abilities by investing in many spiritual and personal development. She loves making unique crystal jewelry designs. Brenda began her intuitive healing journey at a very young age. Learn more at: www.Wellness360Coach.com/brenda-reimer.

SHARON SEABERG

Sharon Seaberg is a Neuro-Transformational Coach™, Feminine Power Facilitator™, Human Design consultant, and founder of the Soul A.L.I.G.N.M.E.N.T. Formula. She empathically fuses cutting-edge neuroscience with intuitive coaching to support open-hearted women to unlock their full potential, live a life of authenticity, and make an impact in the world. Sharon's mission is clear: to support women to find their voice, claim their space, and revel in a life that's meaningful, joyful, and deeply satisfying. Learn more about her transformational services at www.SharonSeaberg.com.

KAREN SHIER

Karen Shier is a midlife transformation guide, Desire Factor and Law of Attraction life coach, energy master, and author who guides women in releasing what no longer lights them up so they can joyfully thrive in their second half of life. She is passionate about supporting women in moving from feeling stuck, stressed, and unhappy to feeling free, empowered, and ready to co-create a marvelous life. Learn more at www.KarenShierCoaching.com.

ABOUT OUR AUTHORS

EFRAT SHOKEF

Efrat Shokef, Ph.D., walks the knowing that everything is possible if we follow our intuition and listen to the signs the universe graciously offers us. She guides parents in parenting from their essence and becoming the humans their children chose to come to. Efrat is a shamanic energy healing practitioner working with children, teens, and families, and the author of *The Promise We Made: Three Universal Soul Promises We Made to Our Children – Near Death Experience and The Parenting Teachings It Invites*. Learn more at www.EfratShokef.com.

BONNIE SNYDER

Bonnie Snyder is an intuitive life balance coach and catalyst. She is a diplomat in energy psychology and a best-selling author. Bonnie is passionate about supporting highly sensitive women, intuitives, empaths, and creatives to let go of limiting beliefs and patterns that hold them back and embrace their sensitivities as the gifts and superpowers they truly are. This unleashes the power to feel empowered and authentic and to fully trust their inner guidance for themselves. Learn more at www.DiamondPathways.com.

About Our Publisher

LINDA JOY

Founded in 2010 by Sacred Visibility™ Catalyst, Mindset Elevation Coach, and Aspire Magazine Publisher Linda Joy, Inspired Living Publishing, LLC. (ILP), is a best-selling boutique hybrid publishing company.

Dedicated to publishing books for women and by women and to spreading a message of love, positivity, feminine wisdom, and self-empowerment to women of all ages, backgrounds, and life paths—Inspired Living Publishing's books have reached numerous international bestsellers lists as well as Amazon's Movers & Shakers lists.

Inspired Living Publishing (ILP) works with mission-driven, heart-centered women entrepreneurs—life, business, and spiritual coaches, therapists, service providers, and health practitioners in the personal and spiritual development genres, to bring their message and mission to life and to the world.

Through Inspired Living Publishing's highly successful sacred anthology division, hundreds of visionary female entrepreneurs

ABOUT THE PUBLISHER

have written their sacred soul stories using ILP's Authentic Storytelling™ writing model and become bestselling authors.

What sets Inspired Living Publishing™ apart is its powerful, high-visibility publishing, marketing, bestseller launch, and exposure across multiple media platforms included in its publishing packages. Their family of authors reap the benefits of being a part of a sacred family of inspirational multimedia brands that deliver the best in transformational and empowering content across a wide range of platforms—and has been doing so since 2006 with the birth of Aspire Magazine.

Linda also works privately with empowered female entrepreneurs and messengers through her Illuminate Sistermind™ Program and other visibility-enhancing offerings. Linda's other inspirational brands include Inspired Living University™, Inspired Living Secrets™, Inspired Living Giveaway™, and her popular radio show, Inspired Conversations. Learn more about Linda's private work and offerings at www.Linda-Joy.com.

Learn how you can be a part of one of our sacred anthologies at **InspiredLivingPublishing.com.**

About Our Editor

DEBORAH KEVIN

Meet Deborah Kevin, founder and Chief Inspiration Officer at Highlander Press, where she channels her passion into empowering changemakers to tell their transformative stories. With a rich background in guiding hundreds of authors from pen to publication, Debby (as she's fondly called) has carved a niche in elevating women's voices through the written word. Her vibrant podcast, STORYTELLHER, serves as a platform to celebrate these voices, fostering a community where every story matters.

Debby's journey is not just confined to the realms of publishing. She's a seasoned traveler, having trekked the Camino de Santiago and explored the world alongside her family. Living in Maryland with her life partner, Rob, and their adventurous puppy, Fergus, Debby infuses her life and work with integrity, curiosity, and a delightful touch of irreverence. At Highlander Press, she's not just publishing books; she's nurturing a movement where every woman's voice is heard, loud and clear. www.DeborahKevin.com

ABOUT THE EDITOR

About Our Editor

LINDA DESSAU

Linda Dessau of LD Editorial has been exploring creativity for many years, from writing stories and singing in choirs to building a thriving music therapy practice. In 2005, she returned to her love for the written word and has since helped dozens of authors and business owners clarify and polish their writing. She is keenly attentive to the author's voice, and to being a collaborative and supportive partner in the writing process. www.LDEditorial.com

www.ingramcontent.com/pod-product-compliance
Lightning Source LLC
Chambersburg PA
CBHW052029030426
42337CB00027B/4920